Confessions
of a
Catholic Worker

Confessions
of a
Catholic Worker

by
Michael Garvey

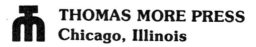

THOMAS MORE PRESS
Chicago, Illinois

ISBN 0-88347-091-8

"The names of those who denounce books should be kept secret."

Moral and Pastoral Theology
by Henry Davies, S.J.
Vol. II, Sec. 4
Sheed & Ward

"The accounts of this vision which reached Constantine cheered him a little, but still he continued to be very anxious."

The Early Martyrs
by Mrs. Pope
Burns & Lambert
London, 1857

INTRODUCTION

There are a few 1968 hippies left. It's true that most of them have become law students, insurance salesmen, movie stars, senators in state legislatures, church bureaucrats, and prayer-breakfast speakers, but scattered among the Newman centers and student unions of American universities is evidence of the survival of the species. As with the black squirrel and the bald eagle of this section of the Mississippi River valley, there is usually something both refreshing and sad about meeting up with them.

I did, recently, meet with a whole colony of holdover hippies in a Newman center near here. There was talk about "action," "dialogue," and, yes, "reappraisals" concerning nearly every political issue from the slaughter of baby seals to the construction of the neutron bomb, but something in the atmosphere of the discussion precluded the old enthusiasms and energies. ("Energy," by the way, seems, in the late seventies, to have replaced "commitment" as the authority upon which just about any action, statement, or point of view can be based. I'm not sure what this linguistic nuance signifies, but there you are.) True, there was no longer the monstrous war in Asia, but there was still a desolate and unreconstructed Vietnamese countryside. True, there was no longer that ruthless and silly investigation of campus radicals, but there was still much to be disclosed about the methods and aims of the C.I.A. True, there was no longer the mining of Haiphong harbor, but there was still the neutron bomb. There was triumph about stopping the B1 bomber (as if this decision had been influenced more by an angry populace than by the cynicism of a few powerful men, taking into account cost-overruns and inflation).

One woman told me that I should visit China and, when I told her that the stuff I'd seen on TV made the People's Republic seem boring, she told me that I was "reactionary." I was alarmed when, in a later context, she remarked that "reactionary elements should be liquidated." She really did! Waiting for her to add something like, "present company excepted, of course," and being disappointed, I asked her if she meant "old fashioned" and "killed." She said, "Yeah, I guess so." I asked her if she'd read Orwell's "Politics and the English Language" (I was showing off). She said she'd never heard of Orwell. *Animal Farm?* Nope. *1984?* Nope. She'd heard of Solzhenitzyn. Solzhenitzyn was a reactionary. And should be . . . ? Yeah.

There was something almost quaint about her dogmatism, and *she* was saying that *I* had been brainwashed by Catholic schools and the middle class. Her approach to everything was like a Marxist version of *The Catholic's Ready Answer*. How someone could flee the Baltimore Catechism to embrace the even narrower *Quotations from Chairman Mao* is beyond me.

But she was, obviously, a special case. She was old fashioned.

Which is why I was surprised when a friend told me that "joining the Catholic Worker movement is an old fashioned thing to do." I think that he said this because he knows, as I do, many people in the movement who joined because of some radical experience or insight undergone in the late 1960s, in the passionate confusion of what has become known as the antiwar movement. Those experiences and insights seem old fashioned now because of something strange that's happened to our sense of history since then. Things that happened less than ten years ago seem as distant from us as the pre-Cambrian era on the geological time scale.

Thank God, the Catholic Worker movement is not nearly as dogmatic as either the Baltimore Catechism or the Little Red Book. If it were, none of the people in this community would be here. If it seems to be, the reason is that it has a developing and articulate social philosophy. The fact that it's concerned with the suffering, oppressed, and poor, with nonviolence and pacifism naturally pleases the philosophy to the left of most political phenomena on this continent, but the philosophy itself stems from orthodox Catholicism, from a belief in the Nicene Creed. The philosophy comes out of a belief, and not the other way around.

And belief is something neither old fashioned nor new, not a good nor a bad idea, but something you live with, like a family or an ingrown toenail. It's also something you live from.

Maybe that's how I wound up at this Catholic Worker house. I've been here a little more than a year, and I have no idea how much longer I'll stay—I may be gone when you read this. But I think I came here because of a belief. That sounds more dramatic than it should. I had a little more say in coming here than I did in getting baptized as a baby, but not all that much. I was raised in a Catholic family and a happy one. We were brought up to believe that it is much better to be in the Church than out of the Church. For me, and for most other people in it, the Catholic Worker Movement, or at least the practice of hospitality, is the best way to experience and express the presence of the Church, the Mystical Body of Christ at work and play in the world. Goofy experiments with the liturgy, boring debates of bishops, we will always have with us, but we also have the Gospels, seven sacraments, the lives of the saints, and a rich tradition. The practice of hospitality is generated by, and brings us closer to all of them. We here are probably the same sorts of Catholic Workers as we are Catholics: sporadically good, sometimes cynical and bad, often indifferent . . . pretty much like everyone else in the Church.

Lord help us all.

I didn't (and none of us here did) graduate from college with the intention of becoming a Catholic Worker. I graduated with the intention of getting out of college, and I succeeded. I worked for a while as a bartender, as a teacher and janitor in a little school in British Columbia, as a janitor at a Holiday Inn, as a clerk in a bookstore, and now I'm here. There was no steady progression, no sudden insight, no conversion, just another nervous and shallow decision, but a good one, I think. If these pages can convince anyone that involvement with the Catholic Worker movement, or at least with the life of hospitality, is not the work of the saints but of everyone, including crazy people and bores, then that will be fine.

Everything described here has actually happened, although in a few places I've compressed things that happened at different times into a single entry, and of course I've changed names in many cases to avoid hurt feelings and arguments. The guy I call here my spiritual advisor really does exist, and I wouldn't reveal his name unless I were tortured. His statements aren't exactly representative of the man, but I thought you'd enjoy them as much as I did.

I've deliberately kept references to fellow staff members to a minimum, which, I'm afraid, might make it sound like I'm the only person working here. That's not at all the case. There are more than half a dozen others on the staff, most of them more involved in the work of hospitality than I am. I love them all enough to be uncomfortable writing about them; I know they'll read this. It's to all of them, Margaret, Dawn, Tom, Bert, Loretta, George, Jack and David, and especially to the late Larry Spiegel, that this writing, with much love, is dedicated.

Lunchtime is crazy.

It's at that time that the anarchy of the Catholic Worker movement bursts into full bloom, and distinctions between staff and guests pleasantly break down. There's no predicting who or how many will come in, who will serve the soup and peanut-butter sandwiches, who will clean up afterwards, and it always seems to be the most enjoyable part of the day.

I prefer to eat in the kitchen, close to the coffee machine and central to the confusion . . . drunks, priests, ex-priests, embittered social workers, pious nuns (one corresponds regularly with Mother Teresa about "our love of the poor and our dear Lord"), Jesus-freaks, junkies, Moonies, Trotskyites, schizophrenics, Jansenists, frightened old ladies, hobos, Knights of Columbus, former monks, building inspectors, pensioners, strident feminists, and tattooed rednecks all eating lunch and arguing about physical resurrection of the body, the possibility of the White Sox taking the pennant, the proper use of Tylenol, stud fees for Triple Crown winners, how to plant onions, the ordination of women, James Joyce, the Tridentine mass, or the population of Shreveport, Louisiana.

In many ways, a microcosm of the Roman Catholic Church.

This place could make me a Catholic chauvinist. All of the strengths and absurdities of our peculiar brand of hospitality would be impossible without the Church, without the two thousand year tradition of a huge, varied, flabby family whose obstinate imagination will always be dissatisfied with the brevity of the Gospels:

> There is much else that Jesus did. If it were all written down, I suppose the whole world could not hold the volumes that would be written.

The ending of John's Gospel might be the thing that drives us nuts. That's why we were told stories about Jesus as a little boy, making birds out of clay and clapping his hands to cause them to come to life and fly away. That's why, in our first grade classroom, there was a picture of the Christ child fleeing to his mother's arms at the sight of a cross surrounded by pink clouds. That's why armed, semipagan adventurers searched for the Holy Grail, and why tormented Midwestern spinsters insist that the Blessed Mother has warned them that Paul the Sixth is an imposter.

The faith which claims that God not only lived fully man in a remote corner of the Roman Empire, but is fully present in bread and wine consecrated every day by his priests, that faith is handling dynamite, and will always flourish in and generate controversy.

The strange meeting, forty-five years ago, of a sharp-minded, revolutionary woman and an eccentric French scholar is, for most people in the Catholic Worker movement, a major event in the two-thousand-year turmoil we call the Church. It's as uneven and diversified as any event in our tradition—a movement impelled by the combination of the naive vision of a fanatic believer and the generous response of a toughminded, practical, good woman. The meeting of these two strange disciples, Dorothy Day and Peter Maurin, started a whole new story among the thousands of stories the gospels have left in their wake. It attracted earnest, joyless people as easily as it attracted clowns and madmen. How completely appropriate for a Catholic enterprise.

Someone once told me a story about a Catholic man who loved architecture. Showing some friends of his around one of his favorite cathedrals, gesturing with delight at the flying buttresses, storied doorways and gothic statuary, he said: "Isn't it wonderful? The Church gives us the wisdom of orthodoxy, the life of the sacraments, the word of God, and all this, too!"

Lunchtime at West Fifth Street evokes something like that peripheral excitement, with all its variety and absurdity. The company of dozens of differently wounded people, the struggles of dozens of equally silly points of view, the sharing and acceptance of dozens of forms of madness place our noon meal in the mainstream of the most misunderstandable of all traditions.

We could all learn a lot from Pete Domino. His unique approach to model-railroading provides him an anchor in the middle of the chaos and outrage of the history of Peter Maurin House. Unswayed by personality cults, fashions, and the zeitgeist, he attends to the construction of his new roundhouse. Unimpressed by bursts of beauty and sanctity (unimpressed, at least, by Teresa of Calcutta), he concerns himself with more gradual curves for his track, since the new Rock Island Line tipped over into Kitty Kat's litterbox. Sudden and direct physical threats temporarily affect him, but within thirty feet of his railroad project, he is confident and defiant as a mother grizzly with her cubs behind her.

So Pete was not, at first, greatly impressed by the formidable John Whitney. John outweighs Pete (who, after swallowing all his railroad equipment and having himself bronzed, would tip the scales at about one hundred) by at least two hundred pounds. He works at the Catholic Worker House by night, and at a rubber processing plant in Rock Island by day. He raises bulldogs, Afghans, and scotties, collects rosaries, scapulars, and miraculous medals, is a superb gourmet cook, embroiders every article of clothing he can get his hands on, studies the Torah in a Rock Island synagogue, faithfully wears his yarmulke (he even went as far as getting recircumcized; I can still startle him by smacking a

meat cleaver on the kitchen table when he's not pay-
ing attention), was once a Benedictine monk, and
has a book of photographs of every species of full-
garbed nun in the U.S.

John lives in a poor section of Rock Island, across
the street from the "Peaches and Cream," a badly
named tavern notorious for violence, bloodshed,
and loud, abrupt noises. John once watched an enraged woman leave the tavern with a large handgun
which she fired six times into the engine of her un-
faithful husband's Cadillac. It's a barbarous and complex neighborhood that John inhabits.

And his house, in the middle of it all, is an oasis of
civilization where the old ways are cultivated. Pen-
zograph sketches of orchids, mattings of fine pictures, chantings of the Psalms, study, great cuisine,
breeding. He shares his small house with his dogs,
his Ethiopian croziers, his chasubles, his rosaries,
and the forests of tropical plants he has accumulated
over the years.

When the house at West Fifth Street is filled to
overflowing, he generously takes home as many
guys as he can fit into his already crowded home,
and they always return bewildered, with Marco Polo
tales of exotic tapestries, rare jewelry, unusual
meals, and beasts unlike any native to the Midwest.

Rennie, John's prize Afghan, was one day badly
in need of relief from the noisy "Peaches and

Cream" area of Rock Island. John had agreed with a Davenport Afghan enthusiast on an attractive stud fee, and wanted Rennie to perform well. Apparently, Afghans are a nervous breed whose lust is easily diminished in a chaotic atmosphere. I haven't yet understood how John came to the conclusion that Peter Maurin House would provide the energizing calm that the dog needed, but at any rate, he appeared in the front hall of the house with the Afghan at his side, and Rennie's vacation immediately got off to a bad start.

The first thing that went wrong was that Pete Domino, railroader, became Pete Domino, burglar alarm. That is not an unusual transition. No one enters or leaves Peter Maurin House unnoticed by Pete. His entire universe is on your left as you walk in the front door, and he conceives each entrance and exit as a potential threat to it. His usual response at these times is to scream the word "Loretta!," the name of one of the three women in the world he does not despise. The other two are Margaret and Dawn, both staff members.

There is usually a silent, assumed (at least by Pete) sentence appended to the initial scream, but its purpose is never the same; variously, "Get 'em outta here," "My Norfolk & Western's broke," "What're they havin' for supper?" "Don't step on the track," "I shit my pants," or "Them goddam women can't leave nothing alone." Infuriated when Loretta, or whoever else is coming in, doesn't answer "Loretta!" the right way, he then flings his door open with a desultory goddammit.

"Goddammit!"

But this time "Loretta" turned out to be an Afghan on the verge of nervous collapse, accompanied by an elephantine ex-Benedictine at least as protective of his dogs as was Pete of his track project. Rennie reacted to the burglar alarm badly, and Kitty Kat, who rarely gets a chance to leave the miniature railroad terminus, who rarely gets a chance to be even slightly assertive, gave pursuit.

The railroad, but little else, remained intact. It looked like Picasso's *Guernica,* all entangled grotesques and hysterical violence: huge ex-monks, startled Afghans, armies of tomcats, furious and emaciated John Henrys. Outrage and chaos.

Pete, from the center of the vortex, screamed that Rennie was a mutt, and there was suddenly an ugly silence.

John will tolerate any insulting reference to himself, and that's a good thing, since there are plenty made around here, but to dispute the ancestry, character, or disposition of one of John's dogs (he calls them his "babies") is to incur the wrath of three hundred twenty pounds of enraged, supermaternal instinct, and that can be nasty.

And it was.

When he saw the look in John's eyes, Pete tried simultaneously to slam the door in his face and to retrieve Kitty Kat, but it was too late. There was too much ex-Benedictine and Afghan in the doorway to allow the door to close.

Domino retreated. Kitty Kat, Rennie, and John advanced.

The terms were orderly and nonviolent. It was quiet inside Pete's room. Only the Railroader and Hassid know what agreement was reached. What everyone else around here now knows is that in John's presence, Pete is as aggressive as a koala bear.

I have it on reliable authority that John Whitney once carried old Harry Allen down the basement stairs to the shower stall. Still, the fact that their combined weights could only be recorded by a weigh-station makes the story difficult to believe. I remember very nearly giving myself a hernia by trying to lift Harry over a curb one afternoon; he'd been trying to return to the Catholic Worker House from halfway down the block. The reason for his rare journey (I had never before seen him go further than the front porch) was a search for the pickup truck he periodically worries about. As far as any of us can tell, the truck is a product of Harry's senility, as are his toolbox, his horses, and his frequent baths.

He's lived at the house almost since its opening, having been brought to the front door by a confused Rock Island cop. It seems that his son had brought the old man to the police station and told the desk sergeant that Harry's senility was too much for him to handle. I've often wondered which aspect of the old guy's eccentricity so annoyed his son. His reluctance to bathe, maybe; or the box of coffee cans filled with epsom salts, spit, Red Man chewing tobacco, safety pins, small hardware, and Kleenex wads. Or Harry's insistence on sleeping fully dressed, complete with corduroy cap and shoes and cane; or his strange diet of oatmeal, prune juice, raw eggs, breadcrumbs, soup-with-sugar, coffee-with-butter. Or his difficult commands like, "Shut off that goddam windmill; them horses don't need no more water. Bury those lightbulbs, Buster!" It could be that the son was exhausted by Harry's endless search for the horses, truck, and toolbox that he's lost somewhere along the way.

It's almost heartbreaking to see how kind the guys at the house are to him, bringing food from the kitchen to his table (the combination of his weight and age makes it difficult for him to walk; a hundred yard dash with Pete Domino and Harry Allen as contestants would take weeks), and stopping to sit and chat with him during the day. The community has accommodated itself easily to his odd habits.

He calls me "the desk clerk," Or, more confusingly, "the man in the chair upstairs." I share the "desk clerk" title with every other male in the house except John—Harry calls John "Missy." John has tried for three years to explain to Harry that his name is John, and Harry has always replied, "That's all right, Missy. Christ sakes, we all gotta get along together here. Why shit?"

To my knowledge, Harry only recognizes Margaret by name. Margaret is the only one of us who can assist him with his Monday bath. Monday, consequently, is Harry's busiest day. His baths were at one time biweekly affairs until John cut his hair one day and found a louse. From first suggestion to emergence from the bathroom, one of Harry's baths is about a two hour project. The first suggestion is invariably answered, "Not today, Margaret. I'm too busy." (This, incidentally, is partly true. Because of his difficulty getting from his bed to the living room with his box of coffee cans, and from the living room to the dining room table where he spends most of the day, and from the dining room table to his bed, Harry's average day is pretty full. Getting his box of coffee cans into the bathroom, getting undressed, and finding misplaced safety pins as Margaret tries to shave him can uncomfortably crowd an already hectic schedule.) But when he finally emerges from the bathroom he is usually invigorated and cheerful, roaring something about being clean as a whistle, ready to roll. "You can just call me Kid Steamshovel!"

Harry Allen ("A-L-L-E-N! Just you ask 'em about me at the Morton Salt Company! Christ sakes amight!") is enraged with Herbert Hoover's ignorance of the working man's life. He stares for hours at the classified section of the Des Moines Register and mutters about how "they" (politicians, I think) are all dirty thieving sonsabitches. He seems happy and contented here, probably thinking that the place is a weird hotel. He and Margaret, says Mr. Allen, have been together for thirty years and more, since they both worked the Mississippi Hotel together. He lives one day at a time, collecting Social Security checks into what must be by now a pretty substantial savings account. His only expenses, after all, are Red Man Chew, Epsom salts, an occasional new cap, or a new pair of pants (with a 50 inch waist and a 28 inch inseam; real crowd pleasers at the laundromat).

At lunch and dinner, Harry eats lightly ("just a halfa bowl for me, Mister!"), subsisting the rest of the day on bowls of oatmeal and mixtures of raw egg and breadcrumbs. The guys wait on him, only occasionally interfering with his diet. Whitey, for example, once prevented Harry from drinking the cup of pink dishwashing liquid he'd poured for himself one afternoon in the back kitchen. Aloysius Grant prevented Harry from eating all the hosts on the paten at the memorial mass for Three-Finger Floyd.

His cheerful disposition is constant, only rarely interrupted by serious and quiet conversations with Margaret about his burial arrangements. She is the only one he'll trust with these. All I know is that he wants to be buried next to his brother Albert (he can't remember his wife's name) in the cemetery behind the Tastee Freeze. "Just you take care of that for me, Margaret, I'll make it all right with ya."

Catholic Workers are anarchists, I'm told, and I wish that I had lots of terrible stories to tell of police brutality on skid row. Unhappily, all my encounters (and most other people's from what I can gather) with the Davenport Police Department have been pleasant. The Davenport Police, for instance, used to buy coffee in shifts for Three-Finger Floyd at the twenty-four hour restaurant he lived in when he was kicked out of our house.

We kicked him out pretty frequently. I saw Floyd sober only once. That was the day he was preparing for one of his monthly court appearances. It was also the occasion of my only coherent conversation with him. About flowers.

Three-Finger (I've never found out how he lost the other two on his right hand) had a degree in horticulture from some Canadian university and was apparently pretty successful in that pursuit before he hit the skids. Even at his drunkest, he retained that enthusiasm, and his appearances at the house with bouquets of stolen lilies were regular. It was an enthusiasm that made him indiscriminate, and incredibly indiscreet. In fact, he once butchered the courthouse lawn, arriving at the house with his floral arrangement only moments before the Davenport Police who graciously allowed Margaret to keep the contraband, but not to keep Three-Finger. During all such appearances, he seldom failed to offend Margaret's feminist leanings by extending the flowers to her saying, "These are for you, Sweetheart. You know, you're awful cute when you're mad."

So generous was Floyd that we found him in the back yard one night, sitting at a picnic table offering a twelve pack of cold beer to an alarmed group of new guys. We'd just read them the riot act about booze in or around the house, and they pretended not to notice Floyd, a pretty difficult thing to do under the circumstances: He was standing them all to a goddam beer, the lilylivered sissies . . . Holy shit (roaring and roaring drunk was Three-Finger) were they all afraid to drink one goddam beer?

You had to love the guy.

But that night notwithstanding, muscatel and white port were Three-Finger's favorites—he was a sort of skid row classicist. I often found him spilling wine all over the floor of the kitchen, swaying, cursing, and insisting that he wasn't drinking. At these, as at most times, his drunkenness made his speech difficult to understand, but his dignity, self-esteem, gallantry, and spirit could always be discerned, no matter how ludicrous his condition.

Fast and cunning was Three-Finger Floyd. One night John kicked him out, realizing too late that during his exit the resourceful wino had grabbed the top (the very expensive top) to John's pressure cooker. By the time John located him, the horti-culturist had arrived safely within the radius of Jake's chain. (In case I haven't explained elsewhere, Jake is our next door neighbor's watchdog . . . a mixture of German shepherd and Idi Amin Dada. It is Jake's custom to eat everything that comes within the radius of his chain; everything, that is, but Three-Finger Floyd, with whom he's established an affectionate relationship. This might be partly due to the fact that the two often slept together in the backyard.)

The exchange was inevitable:

"Three-Finger, you bring that back or I'll break the rest of your fingers."

"Come and get it, asshole."

Floyd was clearly the master of the situation. Even John was cautious about approaching Jake's feeding ground, and Three-Finger was the joyful owner of thirty dollars worth of pressure cooker apparatus. John's first reaction to the news of Three-Finger's death (after his initial dismay had subsided) was, "I'll never know what happened to that pressure cooker top."

On the coldest night of last winter, poor Floyd got too drunk to employ his formidable street-sense. He crawled between two stacks of Babine lumber at the yard on Second Street and froze to death. They called us from the morgue, and Bert drove there to identify the body.

***At the Church of Our Savior in Jacksonville,
Illinois, there is a stained glass window which
depicts Mother Teresa of Calcutta with a
square nimbus above her head.*** You don't see
many square halos these days, maybe because of
the profound mistrust of tradition that seems to be
the spirit of the age. In early Christian iconography,
though, there are lots of examples. The square halo
would be placed over the head of a person the faithful were impatient to exalt. Someone like Teresa of
Calcutta, whose goodness and holiness are legen-
dary, but who hasn't gotten around to death and
canonization as yet.

The square halo has always been unusual because
living people who can sustain the claims we make on
them by calling them saints must be unusual. It could
be that if Mother Teresa lived and worked in Jacksonville, folks there wouldn't be calling her a saint, as
they apparently are now.

The problem with being a living saint (a problem
I'll never have to worry about, so I'm just guessing) is
that there is always someone around who has run
into the darker edges of your sanctity. If, for instance, you'd been the guy who disturbed Francis of
Assisi while he was praying, and Francis had
ordered you to walk naked into a village, preaching
the Gospel (that's a story from the *Fioretti*), you'd
probably think pretty cynical thoughts every time
you walked past a square-haloed birdbath. Or if St.

Benedict had kicked you out of some Egyptian community because you liked to tell jokes; if St. Augustine had said something devastatingly witty about how stupid you were; if you'd been toasted over one of Queen Isabella's purgative bonfires . . . in any of these cases, nobody would blame you for disputing the square halo.

A square halo is at this moment threatening Dorothy Day and the entire Catholic Worker movement, and I think it would be a disastrous blow. Because people within and without the Catholic Worker movement might believe it justified.

Dorothy Day, if she's not a saint, at least speaks with saintly wisdom when she responds to the notion of her own sanctity. She says: I don't want to be dismissed that easily.

Nobody I've met in the Catholic Worker movement does. Nobody should. One of the important challenges to which the movement gives witness is the accessibility and ordinariness of the sort of life it requires. Anyone extroverted enough to be able to answer a telephone fearlessly could accommodate himself to the heroic rigors of the Catholic Worker life. A great deal of the beauty of Peter Maurin's vision of a new society within the shell of the old is its aspect of being no big deal. Life in a Catholic Worker community seems to me no more difficult than life in the most ordinary family—that is, it's immensely difficult.

A searcher for modern sainthood, at least here in Davenport, would be disappointed after about five minutes experience in our house. We're generally rude to the guys, suspicious of newcomers, reluctant (on the rare occasions we're willing at all) to share what we falsely consider "our" time with our guests. The occurrence of the kind gesture, the charitable word, the generous act is as startling, rare, and refreshing here as it would be in the most materialistic and exploitative surroundings. And these gestures, words, and acts are much more often initiated by our guests than by ourselves.

There are, of course, spectacularly good people associated with the Catholic Worker, but the proportion of spectacularly good people is probably just as high at Time-Life Incorporated. Our disadvantage is that people look for spectacular goodness at the Catholic Worker, and not at Time-Life Inc. There is a danger in that self-centered, distracted, irritable, and self-indulgent people with square halos above their heads might obscure their real vision, which is the application of the Gospel to ordinary life.

Somehow, the expression "a bad mood" doesn't seem to fit. I had one of those headaches that makes you accuse someone of buttering toast too loudly. The fact that one of my shoelaces had come untied very nearly reduced me to tears, and my face was wet and sticky anyway. Both my face and my shoelace had wound up that way because it was oppressively hot and humid, a typical Mississippi River Valley midsummer day. The 1964 Chrysler donated to us by a fundamentalist skydiver had run out of gas, and I'd been touring the service stations of downtown Davenport, finding out that gas cans are as rare around here as centaurs. I also just discovered that I had poison ivy. I gave up on the car, and returned to the house for help.

As I climbed the steps of the house, I could hear Andy Whiterock, dead drunk, going into his "everyone hates me 'cause I'm an Indian" rap.

Rene de Voilaume: Faith is the patient work of the will seeking the presence of Christ at all times and in everything.

Exactly, I thought, and once again I've lost faith, because I want to tell Andy Whiterock: "Everyone hates you because you are a pain in the ass." Then I want to tear into tiny threads that flowery burlap poster on the wall that says, "What kind of a revolution would it be if everyone in the world sat down to eat together?" Then I want to wander around downtown Davenport, methodically throwing bricks through gas station windows. Then I'd like to drench both houses in gasoline and ignite them with burning "Ban the B-1 Bomber" leaflets. And take two aspirin and lie down.

It was a good time to call my spiritual director. I called him at his house, where he was trying to figure out how he could list his last trip to Spain as a tax deduction. "Am I ever glad you called just now," he said, "I was thinking about you a moment ago. Do you remember that last line in the 21st Canto of Dante's *Inferno?* I've got it right here, and it goes like this in the Tuscan: 'ed egli avea del cul fatto trombetta,' literally, 'and he made of his asshole a trumpet.' Get it? Satan cuts a fart! I think that's terrific." I had a sinking feeling. We weren't, apparently, going to touch on my problem of faith, and it was my nickel.

Fifteen minutes later, as he was explaining the superiority of Marquis de Riscal to any other rioja (at least for functional purposes), his secretary came in to tell him that the stonecutters' union was on strike. He was furious, since the strike left half the wall of his first grade classroom knocked out. "Say, you wouldn't happen to have any guys up there who used to be masons, would you?" My spiritual director thinks quickly. We didn't. I said goodbye and hung up.

I went directly to Peter Maurin House and took a

cold shower, after which I lay on my bed and let the hot breeze dry me. Thomas Merton died touching a short-circuiting electric fan after showering on an equally hot day. In Thailand or some similar place. What a strange way for such a wise and holy man to go. I brooded about Merton.

And about the Catholic Worker House and about the whole Church. Hans Kung. The Inquisition. Jansenism. Jesuits. Indulgences. The Knights of Columbus. The Papal States. The Curé of Ars. Dorothy Day. Vatican II. The Gospels. The Eucharist.

And about priests. There are priests who drive expensive cars and play golf; priests who seem afraid that you're about to call them "Father"; priests who drink far too much, and priests who don't drink enough; priests who annoy you by trying to convince you that they're just like you by sitting backwards on chairs and wearing ski jackets; priests who condescend and pontificate; priests who don't believe in Christ's presence in the Eucharist; and priests who leave miraculous medals under sofa cushions and dinnerplates. There are priests who build monumental temples, and priests who embroider burlap banners that read, "Jesus makes me feel good." The Church is a leaky vessel, indeed, but for so many of us the only means of transport. That's the problem, or at least, the source of a great deal of annoyance.

The institution drives so many of us crazy because

it is our family and it involves all the joys and embar-
rassments of family life. We talk about its contradictions, absurdities, insensitivities and mediocrities but
these things merely reflect the sluggishness and fear
with which we ourselves respond to the invitation of
Christ: Abide in me.

Finally, we can't be objective about the problems
of the Church because we ourselves are part of the
problems. Somebody once said that papal politics
began two thousand years ago when the first pope
denied three times that he knew Christ. When annoyed with the Pope, we're delighted by the flavor
of the remark, but we are still profoundly close to
Peter in that story. Just as surely as there is no easy
way out of the parable of the Pharisee and the Publican (if we pretend to understand the Publican, we
are being like the Pharisee, and if we know we're like
the Pharisee, we simply know that we're in bad
shape), there is no easy way out of our relationship
to fearful Peter, no easy way out of our relationship
to the Church, no easy way out of our relationship to
Jesus.

And how could any of us be objective about *that*
relationship?

Jesus of Nazareth, Zeffirelli's film disappointed me
because I, like everyone else, know exactly what
Jesus looked like. So does everyone in Italy, and
that's why everyone in Italy argued about it. Apparently, Zeffirelli's film was aired on Italian TV at

about the same time another life of Christ appeared. This one, *Mistero Buffo* (The Comic Mystery), depicts a different Christ from Zeffirelli's more reverent one. I haven't seen it yet, but I hear it presents a Christ who laughs loudly and drinks with his followers, who seems completely at ease during a boisterous and ribald feast at Cana, who is outgoing and gregarious. One of the boys.

The movie caused a furor. Denounced as "blasphemous" by the Cardinal Vicar of Rome, angrily reviewed by *L'Osservatore Romano,* it became the center of controversy, probably between two opposed visions of Christ. Who knows?—the Cardinal Vicar of Rome might be right. It might be blasphemous after all; it might distort the honest and holy effort to understand who this carpenter from Nazareth is. If I saw it, I might be disappointed once again. It wouldn't be my Christ. But the turmoil about this movie is fascinating, energized as it is by one of the oldest and most exciting tensions in the Church.

The debate probably began about ten minutes after the Ascension, and has continued for centuries with theologians on much loftier levels than prime time TV quarreling over where to place the emphasis: Christ's humanity or Christ's divinity.

For many of us, I think, the resolution depends on our mood (and mine, at the moment, is foul). It's irritating to have felt banners with Snoopy cartoons fluttering above you while a condescending young priest gently berates you for believing what a condescending old priest drilled into you when you were seven. At those times, I find myself leaning, perhaps too far, toward Zeffirelli's version. And someday I may be no less startled than the Snoopy people when we both find out how wrong we were.

Association with the variety and strangeness of life here, seeing daily the immense range of human beings who are fascinated and disturbed by the Incarnation, convinces me of the truth in Ezra Pound's lines from "The Ballad of the Goodly Fere":

> They'll no' get him in a book I think
> Though they write it cunningly
> No mouse of the scrolls was the Goodly Fere
> But aye loved the open sea.

The idea is that we're to look for Him in our guests here, and we do as lousy a job, I suppose, as half-hearted Christians everywhere do. What is amazing about even these half-hearted attempts, though, is the generosity with which Christ seems to respond. When we are rude to guests, which is too often, we sometimes see an acquiesence grounded in humility . . . not gutlessness but real humility. When I sullenly hand a bowl of chicken soup to a swaying drunk, who then carefully carries it to chairfast Harry Allen, I am shown a charity which is really redemptive, which throws a light on my own unwillingness to be compassionate.

It's not difficult to understand Peter's reaction to first experiencing the generosity of Christ. His nets were filled to bursting, and he said, "Leave me, Lord, I'm a sinful man." That wasn't being abject, but sensible, in the worst sense of the word. To even attempt to reciprocate that bottomless generosity would have burned him away.

There is the real center of controversy; there is where the Cross is—for a man to sustain, express, and exercise God's infinite generosity simply by sharing God's being, abiding in Him. If you can figure that out, you've got the whole thing knocked. And we're supposed to be like Him for the Kingdom to Come.

Around here, around everywhere, it's easy to see how far away we are from that resolution. Maybe that explains my bad mood.

So we call ourselves members of the Catholic Worker movement. We read the Gospels, and are comforted and terrified.

Events at the men's house on West Fifth are, rightly or wrongly, pretty easy to laugh about. Sometimes I think that if we didn't laugh at them they would overwhelm us. Other times I suspect we may be getting callous.

Often, at Peter Maurin's, our other house, it's not as easy to laugh. We still laugh a lot over here, but there is often something pinched and frightened in the tone of the laughter.

A few minutes ago the Rock Island Police brought to the door a terrified woman, bruised and limping, one eye swollen shut. She'd left her husband and two children in Alabama for an adventurous tour of the North—something right out of a Country-Western song—with a guy who, when they reached the Quad Cities, started drinking a little harder and then beat her up. She managed to get away from him and in touch with the police; they were looking for the guy in another connection, but want her to press charges, too. She won't, because naturally enough, she is intimidated by him—he threatened to kill her children.

Well, the guy's in jail, she's safe here, and the kids are safe in Alabama; but as she climbed the steps of Peter Maurin House this afternoon, she sagged against the railing, burst into tears and moaned, "I'm *so* afraid!" There is something infallible about a statement like that, and there's finally no way to explain it, to put it into the comforting context of societal problems. Her fear and her bruised body and her tears are simply bald, obscene facts.

Battered women are in this year. Suddenly United Fund Committee meetings are swamped with proposals. Programs to deal with this suddenly fashionable problem . . . as if large sums of money, steering committees (whatever they are), outreach (whatever that is), and (I'm not kidding) "raised community consciousness" are going to keep slow-thinking women from accepting abuse and sadistic men from enjoying cruelty.

It is frightening that we never used to hear much about it. What, three years ago, did these women do? Where could they go for help?

I remember one woman who came through here recently. Her husband, she said, would cut her up every time they had sex together. She'd been married to him for ten years and, I suppose, didn't see anything particularly unusual about that. There was something infuriating about her ignorance and passivity. After one lucid moment, she came here looking for help, feeling enormously guilty about having left him. I think she has gone back to him by now.

I admit to a view of the sexes about as primitive as Judaeo-Christian morality and the law of the land allow; to a tendency to see the feminist movement as a luxury, a cause that can only be taken up by a pretty bored and luxurious society. It could be, however, that the feminists' emphasis on what many of us had taken for granted—women are full human beings possessed of all the dignity, potential, and absurdity that men possess—has cleared a space in which confused, stupid, and exploited women can take stock. It could be that without the women's-rights-rhetoric which bores so many of us, women and men alike, more of these tortured and abused people would simply accept their affliction as a fact of life.

The lady from Alabama is sleeping right now, exhausted from pain and fear. She gave us a number in Alabama where her husband can be reached; he's always been very kind to her, she says, and we're all praying she's right. He'll be coming tomorrow to take her home.

A local disc jockey who has been saved comes occasionally to the bar where I work to drink Creme de Menthe on the rocks and to argue with me. He has helped me put my finger on what drives me, and lots of others, crazy about born again Christians. "I was in the dark for so long," he said, "until the day I met Jesus. Now everything's clear. I know I'm saved." His enthusiasm, his dedication, his genuine joy . . . these are impressive. His glibness is not.

To hear him talk about Jesus, you would think that Our Lord approached Jerusalem forcing himself to keep a straight face. As if he knew that his passion and death were to be a historical prank played on foolish mankind, a sort of practical joke whose punchline would be an empty tomb. I once heard an ex-seminarian who had overdosed on theology say much the same thing. We can't deny the humor of the whole story, he said. Maybe so. If, that is, God's sense of humor is anything like ours in our strangest moments. At any rate, to see the comedy in the Agony at Gethsemane is a vision of which most of us are incapable.

I don't at all mean to dismiss the faith of evangelical Christians. The disc jockey with whom I argue about these things is a man who has definitely begun to direct his life away from himself, toward a new intensity, a deeper dimension. But there is a very real danger that the slick approach to Truth of the 700

Club Jesus-people could become, or already is, an urge of mere flesh. Flesh, after all, means something far more than that confusion of dirty thoughts that Sister Mary Agnes warned me to avoid. The urges of the Flesh are simply the demands made upon us by a world that does not acknowledge the Kingship of Christ. I succumb to the flesh perhaps even by being practical when God wants me to be reckless, by hesitating to encourage a bore, by making a visit to a church when I should be welcoming Christ in the person of an annoying teenager.

I'm uncomfortable hearing people talk about the mission upon which Christ has sent them. Maybe the real mission is to be silent about Christ, and alert to his directions.

I agree with my friend that to be a Christian is to be confronted with a real person, but I think that, as in a love affair, a marriage, or a street fight, confrontation is only the beginning, and far from the end, of a long series of problems.

Transactional analysis, astrology, the Unification Church, EST, the waves of self-help, self-discovery, self-congratulatory books . . . all of these phenomena have provided our time with about as boring and depressing a vision of our possibilities as the flesh can provide. The Good News won't quietly take its place in these ranks, but will challenge them. The problem with the attempt to furnish Christ with a leisure suit is that, once the subject is brought up, he might demand to go naked.

Ours *is* a joyful religion, holding a promise beyond our imaginings, but the promise is only to be attained after a dreadful struggle with everything we are now comfortable with, including ourselves; the joy to which we are called is a fierce thing, something which in our present state we couldn't sustain.

Anthony Bloom, in his great book, *Meditations: A Spiritual Journey Through the Parables,* quotes an arresting passage from a story of Hermas the martyr, whose guardian angel speaks to him of the apparent ruthlessness of God's love. "Be of good cheer, Hermas," the angel says, "God will not abandon you before He breaks either your heart or your bones!"

Whenever I go into the Davenport Library, the librarian in the record section asks me about Tommy, a mutual friend and an occasional guest at our house. Sometimes she just asks: Is our friend still working on his Vietnamese? He made a big impression on her. She was witness to the earliest symptom of Tommy's madness; he'd come into the library on a very hot day, wearing his raincoat and red stocking cap, to listen to the Davenport Library's only Teach-Yourself-Vietnamese record which, he said, might save his life some day.

He was going to work for the C.I.A.

Tommy's sudden career choice wouldn't have been as strange if it hadn't been made after a long period of average skid-row life. Compared to many of the guys, Tommy was pretty normal. Compared to, say, Bob, who always wore four belts and thought that we had sent his jockey shorts to Iowa City to be analyzed, Tommy was an aristocrat of sanity.

But soon after he announced he would sign on with the C.I.A., he flipped out completely. So completely that he shouted, nonstop, for at least six hours, from the time he stormed out of the house leaving an untasted bowl of vegetable soup and a peanut butter sandwich behind until three policemen, an orderly, and two nurses strapped him to a bed at Mercy Hospital. The intensity of his vision and the urgency of his message left him no time for silence, and, even as the soft leather straps were being tightened around his wrists and ankles, Tommy continued to threaten, prophesy, exhort, promise and pray.

It was not simply the misery of germs, filth, sin, chaos, cruelty, indignity, and murder that tortured him . . . it was, he screamed at us, the policemen, and hospital personnel, his position in the universe. He had pleaded, Lord, how he'd pleaded, to be allowed to die, allowed to rest; but no, he must carry the message on, even if none would listen, even if he were met (as we around his shaking bed met him) with infuriating sympathy. He was a C.I.A. agent, and knew of a hydrogen bomb in the Quad Cities area about which he'd tried to warn the Civil Defense people, who wouldn't listen. There had been an explosion in the atmosphere which was at that moment grilling us all with million degree heat. He was a prophet who gave the world until 10:00 the next morning before "the bad folks would wish they'd never been born, but for the good it will be a fine spring day." He was the Son of God and must die once more. He breathed fire and should not be touched.

Chesterton says somewhere that the problem with a madman is not that he has lost his reason, but that he has lost everything else but his reason. And we all came smack up against that problem as we stood stupidly around poor Tommy's bed, assuring him

that the bonds were for his own good (instead of telling him the truth: that the bonds were for *our* own
good) and being made even more obviously foolish
by his arguments. If he actually were the Son of
God, he probably would wind up in the same position, or a worse one.

At any rate, over the next few days, Tommy's
rage mellowed until it no longer exceeded Iowa law's
requirement for involuntary commitment: that the
crazy person's condition not be "a threat to himself
or to others." He left the hospital mildly dazed and
with little recollection of the hydrogen bomb and his
messianic mission. I recently saw him over near
Credit Island, walking along the highway in a Con-
federate cavalry hat carrying a two-by-four.

The rebel. Who can blame him for finally putting
his foot down? The neighborhood he shares with us
would put anyone in a defensive posture. Right
across the street from the scene of his interception by
the Davenport police, an evangelical bookstore dis-
plays a picture of a terrifying Jesus overlooking a col-
lapsing Davenport downtown—buses collide with
cars, buildings burn and crumble, river-barges sink in
flames, and from the local holocaust about a dozen
winged and faded members of Davenport's Elect as-
cend towards a hideous savior. Underneath the picture, inscribed in gaudy, flaming typeface is the
message: "Jesus is coming." Half a block down the
street from behind the front window of a massage

parlor, a blue rabbit with spectacles and tiny antlers looks out at potential customers. A comic-book-style balloon over the rabbit's head promises new girls, lower prices, and air conditioning. On a day as hot as the day Tommy flipped, harsh sunlight accentuates splintered wine bottle fragments and the bizarre tattoos of shirtless winos.

Who can blame poor crazy Tommy for wanting to descend from the skies with H-bombs to blow it all away?

Overdoses of Catholic Worker rhetoric sometimes tempt us to believe that nearly everything that goes wrong with psyches, bodies and souls is the result of what Dorothy Day, with her customary bluntness, calls "this filthy, rotten system." But it's possible that the emphasis of that rhetoric distorts our perception of another dragon. This dragon may not be on intimate terms with Madison Avenue, Pentagon financing, corporate greed, or national bloodlust; it may be freelance.

Peter Maurin and Dorothy Day started a movement with the holy task of doing battle with an evil system, and in this battle, as, I suppose, in all battles, there are surprises. Tommy was a surprise for all of us. Maybe the attempt at some sort of reconnaisance of his suffering strains our equipment too greatly. Maybe to ask "Why?" is to ask too much.

His Beautitude and Eminence Thomas Cardinal Brennan is a difficult man to describe. He's a university graduate, an ex-marine, a veteran of World War II, a former career man, a southside-Chicago Catholic, father of seven, former Salvation Army truckdriver, sometime Catholic Worker guest, lover of children, lover of dogs, fierce opponent of freethinking, anti-communist, beer-lover, White Sox fan, balding, irritable, compassionate.

We used to call him, simply, the Monsignor. I'm not sure just when he was elevated to the College of Cardinals. (When addressed with his new title, he responds angrily, "If I don't get no raise, I don't want no promotion.")

Tom Brennan lives by himself in a boarding house not far from here, supported by a variety of spot labor and truckdriving jobs, separated by a series of vague and unfortunate incidents from his family. We are happy and privileged to be a surrogate. I'd rather go to a Trini Lopez concert than tell him this, but he's among the kindest, most generous people I've ever met and an indispensable friend of our community.

He knows that; we know that. No one admits it.

He calls us crazy commies and describes the *Catholic Worker* as "that pinko magazine" even while he's helping us distribute it. To Tom the notions of voluntary poverty and voluntary strangulation make about equal sense. Says the Cardinal, "There sure as hell is nothing voluntary about mine!"

And that's true. He thinks we're all nuts, thinks that we should all get "real" jobs and do "real" things. Still, in the middle of his own misfortunes, Brennan conducts a grumbling and cranky ministry, although he'd be mortified to find that out.

Once he asked for an extra container of soup after lunch: "There's this goofy sunuvabitch staying at the Dempsey," the Cardinal growled, "the idiot's been on a bender for two weeks, and, like I got some time to kill, so I thought I'd go down and get him to eat something." He added, probably suspecting that someone would accuse him of being kind, "What the hell, the sunuvabitch owes me five bucks, and if I don't slow him down, he's gonna run outta money!"

Brennan worries deeply about the entire population of Davenport's skid row, about the staff of the Catholic Worker House, about the strange people who visit here. He visits guys in the hospital and in nursing homes; takes people food; freely shares the little money he makes at odd jobs; and spends nearly all his free time at the house helping us. A cranky, heavydrinking, obstinate version of St. Francis, if he read this his first reaction would be, "Whatta crocka bullshit!"

I assume this because I'm sure that his reaction to praise would be much like his reaction to any hint of affection; once I was, very reluctantly, involved in a complicated and potentially violent family dispute. A friend and I had to go to the house in which all of this complication and violence was centered, and Brennan thought we were nuts. (I did, too, of course, but was vain enough not to admit that I was terrified.) "Lemme know when you're going over there," the Cardinal snarled. "You people are nuts to get involved with these crazy spade family rows. If that coon gets rough, I'd like to be around. After all, I know you're an asshole, but we've kinda gotten used to ya."

Obviously, to have had Brennan along, with all of his deep loyalties and prejudices, would have been about as comfortable as escorting Anita Bryant to a gay bar. We didn't tell him when we were "going over there." But I was astounded by his concern.

Later, when we returned, having completely failed to resolve the family problem, but having delightedly succeeded in keeping ourselves intact, I told Tom with great relief that I was OK.

The Cardinal's response: "yer *what* hurts?"

I forget what I answered, but the embarrassing suspicion of affection between us, to our mutual satisfaction, immediately vanished as a result.

5-7   work in the fields
7-9   Mass
9-10   breakfast
10-11 lecture or discussion
11-2   rest or study
2-3   lecture or discussion
3-4   cold lunch
4-5   lesson in handicraft
5-8   work in the fields
8-9   dinner
9-5   sleep

Who can doubt that Peter Maurin was an idealist? The schedule above is one of his blueprints for life on an ideal farming commune. For even the most enthusiastic *Foxfire* reader, or for the most unimaginative Maoist, it could make life even duller, more joyless, and more routine than a summer session in a parochial grade school.

Happily, there are few, if any, Catholic Worker houses or communes which follow his plan, just as there are few (I only know of one, offhand) Benedictine monasteries which follow the Rule. If you were to confine yourself to this schedule, the moments during which you teased cats, discovered how long you could hold your breath, stood on your head, smeared pennies on railroad tracks, shuffled cards, or shot rubberbands at flies would be confined to three hours in the middle of the day. No pizza in this schedule; no movies; no imitations of absurd bishops.

But certainly, Maurin never intended to be destructively specific about the outward forms of the sort of society he envisioned, as St. Benedict apparently did. He fired his blueprints and Easy Essays against the barbarism of a neopagan age like a man shooting a slingshot against Sherman tanks. He was aiming, I think, for any dramatically Christian opposite to a deliriously greedy and powerful society. He was a romantic.

And, as with any romantic, it's easy to misunderstand and laugh at him. His excesses are like St. Paul's, the results of a crowded schedule. St. Paul thought that everything was going to end (or begin, depending on your point of view) before the ink had dried on the pages of his epistles. Peter Maurin realized that "we are parked in a dead alley."

I'm sure that I can't even begin to understand the selfless life of this complicated and saintly man, but I felt close to an understanding of him when I read Dorothy Day's obituary of him in the June, 1949 issue of the *Catholic Worker*. It's reprinted there from time to time (the last I know of is June, 1977) and is indispensable for an understanding of the Catholic Worker movement.

I know a man who met Peter Maurin when he read some of his Easy Essays at the University of Notre Dame. "He was a kook," the man said, and then quickly added, "the way St. Francis of Assissi was a kook. A holy kook."

I'm not sure where the Christmas tree came from. It was probably donated, like the cookies and turkey which are annually brought to the house by angry-looking Girl Scouts. (Our house, itself, is not particularly squalid, but I think that the beaten-up look of lots of our guests scares the girls a little and makes them scowl as they sing "Joy to the World.")

The tree was definitely a beauty. It dwarfed the living room, where we placed it. John assumed command of its decoration, marshalling the talents of the guys as they strung popcorn and threw tinsel, solving wiring problems with strings of Japanese-made Christmas-tree-lights. Occasionally, he'd let slip some dark grunt about "crazy goyim" or "it's just another day on the calendar."

We took pictures of the guests and ourselves standing around the tree. There was Al, who had fled to Muscatine after having been deserted by his wife in Biloxi. He was from Alabama, and, in an accent that made Merle Haggart sound like Alistair Cooke, would do painstaking, endless imitations of Elvis Presley and Jerry Lee Lewis, patiently accompanied by crazy old Aloysius Clarence Grant, who would play at these times the only chord he knew over and over again on Dawn's guitar. It was difficult to work in the kitchen and maintain a straight face whenever Al's poor mother called him on the phone; they would debate in detail the origins and possible resolution of Al's marital problems.

(Privacy, if I haven't mentioned it yet, is a big problem here. Overcrowding places any phone call, from news of a tragic death to the pledging of undying love in center stage.) "Ma, the way I see it, you gotta live your life and we gotta live ours . . . I know, I know, but she throwed a bucket'a milk on me, so I swung a fryin' pan at . . . I don't give a good goddam what the judge says and I'll tell him that to his . . . now don't be ignorant, Ma, this is a Catholic place and these . . . but I'll just be here till I get back . . . I know, and I like peach melba as much as the . . . oh, Ma, goddamit . . . ."

We would try to talk to anyone passing through the kitchen, to bang pot lids, to have other things to do at other places in the house, but it was impossible to avoid overhearing Al's byzantine analysis of family suffering.

There was Nick, who arrived two or three days before Christmas (yes, *Nick*) with rimless, half-moon glasses, a red stocking cap, and a large gunny-sack which he carried Santa-Claus-style over his right shoulder. He was a silent, mysterious man, who spoke—only when someone else spoke to him—in whispered monosyllables as he patiently threaded particles of popcorn for the tree. We never decided whether Nick was an archangel or Santa Claus, but the mystery was deepened when he left on the 24th with "some things to do," returning on the 26th having been "around." His gunny-sack was empty, by the way, when he came back. Aside from compulsively cleaning everything in the house, and shoveling snow (every sidewalk and driveway for two blocks in all directions), Nick's specialty was obtaining rancid meat from the garbage cans of a neighboring German restaurant and feeding it to Shanti, our cat. The abrupt change in Shanti's diet left devastating results under Larry Spiegel's bed, where the cat usually slept, but none of us could bear to suggest to Nick that he find another outlet for his charity. Besides, he disappeared by New Year's Day.

There was Jimmy (he would call himself "Dimmy") who celebrated Christmas (Chwismas) in his stocking feet (weet) because of a severe staph infection, which he discovered and displayed in the kitchen at precisely the moment I'd bitten into a custard-filled sweet roll, thus permanently enshrining himself and his feet (weet) in my memory.

There was Dan Ryan, a massive, silent, slow-moving black man, thoroughly unemployable because of his sluggishness. He was an avid reader of Zane Grey westerns and the Book of Revelation, and one evening put lumps in everyone's throat by stealing a missalette from St. Anthony's Church, shyly suggesting that we read the Collect for the day's Mass instead of grace. The only other time I saw Dan Ryan overcome his shyness was when, at grace before dinner, he requested prayers for his friend, Larry Spiegel, who had died at our house that morning.

There were a dozen others around the tree: Todd, the lanky cook from Worcester, Massachusetts, who stayed at our house between binges and made John a little jealous by cooking highly-praised meals. It was Todd who first noticed that John Meslin (or Hardrock Kid, King of the Hobos) was having a heart attack early one morning. The king survived, and is in our group-portrait, complete with Amish, broadbrimmed hat, blue overcoat, white gloves and Bat Masterson cane. And Aloysius Clarence Grant, crazy and one-eyed, topped with an amputated stocking to mold his diminishing Afro. (John had cut Aloysius' hair a few days before. He told him that it was an easy job, since he was already proficient at clipping toy poodles.) It was a scene to dismay a cartoonist.

But Christmas Day was depressing. Upstairs, the record player boomed at full volume the King's Chapel Cambridge Choir singing "Hodie Christus Natus Est." Downstairs men chainsmoked cigarettes and stared out the front window at Fifth Street slush. Al attempted, and gave up on, an imitation of Elvis Presley's "Blue Christmas." Sporadic, phony bursts of cheerfulness exploded throughout the house, making the enveloping silence twice as uncomfortable. And empty.

A few of the regulars, crushed by voluntary or involuntary separation from wives and families, didn't even show up, trying to stay as drunk as possible until the joyful season ended.

I kicked a guy out.

He was a usually calm Mexican kid named Tony, who showed up Christmas morning completely smashed. Grabbing a butcher knife, he started to carve up a donated ham while he picked a fight with Lou, another guest who was growing more and more sullen as the lonely morning grew longer and longer. He left quietly; Christ expelled from our midst.

We'd put together little token presents for the guys, wrapped in *Catholic Worker* back issues and dressed up slightly with green and red yarn and magic marker decorations. We put the presents under the tree, around the creche. Mostly candy, shaving stuff, tube socks, and cigarettes. Someone had suggested after-shave lotion, and someone else had mentioned that many of the buys would be desperate enough to drink it. Someone else had said to hell with it, let them drink the crap if they want it so badly. Nobody got after-shave lotion.

Hodie Christus Natus Est. The joy of the Incarnation renews the whole world. The rose from root of Jesse. The glad tidings. I tried to think about the Good News, about happiness in the center of squalor . . . the first Christmas, about Christ coming once again and forever to all of us bums, cynics, weirdos, winos, rich, and poor.

But it was impossible to get a fix on the Child in the manger. There was only this sad stable.

I couldn't wait for Christmas to be over. Neither could anyone else. The atmosphere the next morning was one of quiet triumph, as if a suffering had been endured and survived.

Few of our guests have been as widely liked and enthusiastically received as Pepper. He was another kind of outcast, having been rejected even by a religious community. St. Ambrose Seminary does not allow its students to keep dogs.

Pete Domino could, and often did, get away with calling Pepper a mutt. Pepper was an amalgam of terrier, dachshund, beagle, Labrador, collie, and Newfoundland. He was referred to us by his master, Greg, a seminarian who'd decided that the pace and variety of our communal life would further broaden his outcast dog's already considerable experience. Recklessness and wanderlust were Pepper's salient attributes, and he'd left traces of his ancestry all over the Quad Cities. He was one of the only members of our community unimpressed with the ferocity of the Martinez' watchdog Jake, who lived next door. He was often seen lifting his leg inches away from the perimeter of Jake's chain (and this, even after the chain snapped one morning, and Pepper survived only through the courageous interference of two talented hobos and a chicano grandmother).

We'd warned Greg that we'd had a lousy history with dogs. Kilty, our last one, had been kidnapped by a sullen family of hillbillies, and his three or four predecessors had been even less fortunate. But for some reason, we all assumed that Pepper's elasticity, cunning, experience, and sense of irony would be defense enough against the sorts of dangers and disappointments that had confronted Kilty, John's Afghans, bulldogs, and Scotties in the past.

We were wrong. Pepper had been with us for about five months when, accompanying Margaret and me on an evening walk, he managed to get himself crushed by a carload of baseball players. After an ugly thirty seconds or so, he yelped his last, and passed on, as had the impolite athletes. Margaret hurried back to the house to notify Greg and to get the truck, while I stayed behind to watch the corpse.

Pepper came home wrapped in a baby blanket which John and I had swung, sniffling and reassuring each other that it was just a goddam dog, into the back of the pickup truck. Most of the guys staying at the house knew and liked Pepper. They interrupted their TV watching to file past the truck for a last look. We were most worried about Larry, who'd grown very close to Pepper over the last few months. Larry moaned that he'd lost his best friend, which hurt Margaret's and my feelings. He apologized, and we hauled the heavy blanket out to the back yard: first Bert and Larry with the deceased, then John, Margaret, and I, with flashlights, spade, and potato fork, then four or five close friends, and finally the Archbishop.

The Archbishop is an eccentric named Vittorio who passes through here from time to time, usually carrying stacks of brochures describing everything from the slaughter of baby seals to the possibility that Cardinal Suenens is a Freemason. Always resplendent with pectoral crosses and holycards and anti-B1 bomber buttons, he once offered Dawn his hand in marriage. She gently refused him.

As the Archbishop began Pepper's eulogy, Margaret and John began an argument. Someone at the back of the crowd had callously suggested that we put Pepper to good use, burying him as close as possible to the tomato plants which were faltering in the hot-box. John thought that it wasn't such a bad idea, but Margaret insisted that *she* wanted to be buried there when her time came. Things grew louder and more confusing as the argument competed with the Archbishop's eulogy, and the Martinez family next door began to gather on their back porch, wondering why Jake was barking so hysterically.

What they saw in the backyard of the Catholic Worker House probably appeared to them to be the liturgical finale of a ritual infanticide, and I became afraid that they were thinking that the flipped-out Anglos next door were celebrating a black mass. (Grandma Martinez did seem a little reserved for the next few days.)

John and Margaret finally compromised, the Archbishop completed his eulogy, and the digging began. As most of the mourners dispersed, Larry and

I started carrying rocks from the vacant lot behind Peter Maurin House to build a mound over the grave. We'd both seen that done in Westerns before, and it seemed appropriate. The Martinez family watched us in silence.

Since then, many of us have grown more affectionate toward Jake, perhaps as emotional therapy after Pepper's abrupt passage. It occurs to me now that there are a number of guys staying at the house who never knew Pepper. In fact, the night Jake was arrested and taken to the pound (for observation after his attempt to eat the thigh of a slow-moving and startled dinner guest) I noticed a hobo sitting on top of Pepper's rockheap, eating his dinner, apparently unaware that he was enjoying his pork and beans above the mortal remains of a former guest.

**At Mass today, we celebrated the mystery of
the Trinity.** The strange belief that there are three
persons in one God, the priest told us, is undeniably
central to our faith. And it is a revelation that came in
time, with the coming of the Messiah. At the house
of Caiphas, he told the High Priest, "From now on,
you will see the Son of Man seated at the right hand
of God, and coming on the clouds of heaven." That,
to Caiphas, was infuriating, blasphemous.

The charge of blasphemy is still another difficult
thing in the New Testament. It's easy to forget, or
overlook, the fact that many of those who charged
that Jesus was a blasphemer must have made that
accusation in good faith. There must have been
many good and holy men, genuinely and unselfishly
worried that this new teacher was undermining the
faith they loved, paving the way for a massive per-
secution of their people, his own people.

"Hear, O Israel, the Lord your God is One!"
That's not an easy claim to dismiss. Wise and pious
men rebuked Christ with it. Centuries later, whole
families chanted it as they confronted the ovens of
Auschwitz. Moses became a gigantic figure in the
history of faith because he would not compromise,
because he insisted that Abraham's wandering de-
scendants, Christ's ancestors and ours, must not pay
homage to dozens of local deities. The Jews must
have seemed an odd and dangerous people to those
who encountered their loyalty to the one God whose

name was so sacred that it could only be whispered by priests in the Holy of Holies. It was a conviction that must touch every aspect of life, and the morality and customs to which it gave rise made them seem strange to their easygoing pantheist neighbor.

In this neopagan age, when even the claim that there is no God betrays unfashionable enthusiasm (who was it who defined "negative capability" as "the deliberate ending of all those boorish longings for eternal verities"?) the Christian belief that Jesus is Lord should make us even stranger to our neighbors. Jesus, our Lord and brother, who taught us that through the power of the Holy Spirit we could call God, not by his sacred name, but by Abba. Pappa. Daddy. We could become one with him, through the Spirit. One with God.

It was a hot day, and all of us dozed during the sermon. The priest delivered it in a flat monotone, barely distinguishable from the offertory hymn. We received communion, sang a song together and left.

Back at the Catholic Worker House, John was making French toast for the guys. I yelled at Maynard for taking more than two pieces. There wasn't enough syrup to go around, either.

I hold the record for escape attempts.

There was going to be a meeting of Clergy and Laity Concerned in Cleveland. I was sick of the house, and my sister lives in Ohio, so I offered to drive Margaret to the event. We started off enthusiastically, she talking about nonviolent workshops, and I about clean bathrooms. I had nothing against the meeting, but had no intention of going to it. I wanted to drink bourbon and gossip with my family.

I was wrong, I know. My concern should have been the poor and oppressed instead of good meals and stories. As if to emphasize how wrong I was, our car died on a quiet stretch of Illinois prairie heavily populated by Polish Catholics. It didn't malfunction or break down, it died, or so the mechanic told us. Something like a Johnson rod being throwed and bartacking an overwinch, thereby reaming a jack-bearing and freezing out the quarterframe. We nodded solemnly, pretending to have a vague idea what the guy was talking about, and decided to sell the car for scrap metal (to a smug, leisure-suited fat guy in a carpeted office; over his desk was a bronzed shovel inscribed, "If you can't wow 'em with wisdom, baffle 'em with b——t") and take whatever we could get.

It was only a baby, by our standards—108,000 miles. Still, we made just about enough money to buy a good, used bicycle tire. We were miles away from anywhere. The Interstate was rumored to be at least a dozen miles away from the garage, and it was starting to snow heavily. Margaret remembered a friend of hers, a pastor in the area.

It was embarrassing, but she placed a call to him, asking him if he'd be good enough to drive over, pick us up, and give us a ride to the Interstate, on which we could easily hitchhike back to Davenport. An astonishingly kind guy, he said he was delighted and was on his way.

From the speaker of a poorly tuned transistor radio, Johnny Cash was singing "Big River" and mechanics festooned with elaborate tattoos were sympathizing with us about the fatally throwed Johnson rod when our rescuer arrived.

I will never understand how such a variety responds to the priestly vocation. Once I met a priest from a small parish in Southern Illinois who'd been thrown out of a bar after starting a brawl with some coal miners, parishioners of his. It was never made clear whose fault the brawl was. When I was in the first grade, the pastor of our parish preached a sermon at a man's funeral, thumping the closed lid of the coffin and yelling, "It's too late for Arthur!" He was a forceful, imaginative man, who claimed that if you were left handed, you were probably possessed by the devil, and that we should all be thankful "because you all could have been born niggers!" Then there's Pope John the 23rd. Or Daniel Berrigan. Or Andrew Greeley, the Curé of Ars, Theodore Hesburgh, Camillo Torres, Hans Kung, Edmund Campion, my spiritual advisor, St. Peter, and this guy, our rescuer, another extremist.

A kind man, and eager to help us in any way possible, he skipped into the garage, completely cowing the mechanics, who retreated immediately to the other side of the dead car. They stared as he and Margaret greeted each other. He wore his collar all right, but with an immaculate black suit (which I later discovered he'd made himself) of crushed felt. A medallion dangled between his lapels, an intricately wrought silver fish with a rhinestone eye. His hair was slightly grey and carefully coiffured, like an art museum curator's. Nobody could figure him out.

What was easy to figure out was his goodness. He seemed at least as disappointed as we were about the death of the car, insistent upon giving us money, and reluctant to let us hitchhike back. He wanted to drive us to a bus station and buy us tickets. He wanted to give us more money, food, a car, anything. We persuaded the good man to drop us off at a convenient exit on the westbound Interstate. (About a week after we returned, he sent a check to the house, a very generous check.)

We got one ride from a black guy on his way to Geneseo to visit his girlfriend. He drove steadily in his C.B. equipped Cadillac ("pretty bad ride, dontcha think, Bro?") at 90 miles an hour. His handle was Superfly. From Geneseo to the Quad Cities, we were driven by a bowhunter recovering from a motorcycle accident which had taken place on the night he divorced his wife. We thought *we* had troubles.

West Fifth Street smelled familiarly like urine, socks, and cigarette smoke. John was baking blueberry muffins in the kitchen. Old Harry Allen was either vomiting or spitting chewing tobacco into his Folger's coffee can. Carrack, as usual, was drunk. He asked how the meeting was, and I growled at him.

We were home again.

The polar bear, next to man, is the most dangerous beast in a survival situation. (I don't speak from experience, of course, but on the authority of a survival manual I read while sitting in an easy chair.)

Apparently, the bear attacks anything which moves on the level polar ice. It says in the manual that the whiteness of the bear makes him nearly invisible, but that if you're lucky enough to have spotted him before he's devoured you, and lucky enough to have had the foresight to bring along a powerful rifle, the best way to deal with the beast is to shoot him. (Or her.)

The Judaeo-Christian tradition does not allow this approach to the many political mavericks who are, for one reason or another, drawn occasionally to our house. So often, though, they resemble polar bears in their aggressive posture towards anything that moves to the right or to the left on their political horizons. Tradition, and the fact that we couldn't find a powerful rifle, saved one such visitor the other night.

Could she ever talk. People in my family tell me that I'm a compulsive talker, but I'll bet if I'd returned that night from a Trappist monastery after having been given an injection of amphetimines, I couldn't have kept up with her monologue . . . about women's rights, gay rights, the Nestle's boycott, the Stevens' boycott, her last boyfriend's sexism, macrobiotics, macrame, women's ordination, ordination, EST, sisterhood, brotherhood, vegetarianism, chiropractery, and monosodium glutamate. I tried to keep up with her, got exhausted, and left. I hadn't spotted the bear in time.

Hiding in my room at Peter Maurin house, I started to read Tom Klise's novel *The Last Western*. It was appropriate and refreshing, in the wake of that verbal storm, to read about the Silent Servants of the Used, Abused, and Utterly Screwed Up. That's the name of an ascetic religious order which the book's hero joins to fight the bleakness and hopelessness of an only slightly fictitious future world.

"Canonically speaking," says a Vatican spokesman, "they're nowhere." Of course they're nowhere. They never say anything. Each novice in the order is given two books which are to be read in silence. (Everything is to be done in silence, and all communication is through sign language, since words have proven to be for the most part lies and sins in this future world.) The two books are the New Testament (newly entitled "Hints") and a brief history of the Silent Servants ("Lesser Hints"). Not a bad idea.

If there is to be a new, Franciscan sort of movement in the Church—and the best elements in the Catholic Worker movement promise one—maybe it should be silent. What if St. Francis had been born in the late 1940s? He'd probably be invited to speak on the panels of the Johnny Carson Show, the 700 Club, and Tomorrow. St. Francis with Ed Mc-Mahon, Jerry Lewis, and Johnny Carson:

Johnny: Frank, tell us about some of that marvelous work you do.

Francis: It's not really work; we give what we have to the poor, own nothing, and follow Christ.

Johnny: I think that's wonderful. If more people had your courage and warmth, the world would be a really wonderful place (nodding gravely and turning a twitchy face to the applauding audience). Don't you all think so?

Jerry Lewis: And Frank, don't you think it's very rewarding, too? My kids' eyes just light up when I tell them about the wonderful stuff that people like you and the folks who support the March of Dimes (acknowledging applause) . . . and it just makes me vewy vewy (making a cute, little boy face) happy to think that there are lots of young people, like you, Frank, who are willing to give up their time . . .

Simple, profound love would be discerned as a challenge to structures, a new ethnic movement, a filler between denture-cleaner commercials, a reaction to this, a response to that . . . always filtered, distilled, adulterated by the worldly artifice of language. ("Francis, do I hear you saying that we should follow Christ in a faith context, or in the theology of liberation paradigm?")

> Plain 'Yes' or 'No' is all you need to say; anything beyond that comes from the devil.
>
> (Matthew: 5;37)

Those of us who worry about the Church (or, for that matter, anything else) could learn a lot from the simplicity to which Christ exhorts us in the sermon on the mount. It could well be that the choice between plain "Yes" or "No" goes beyond language, beyond the taking of an oath right to the heart of our relationship with Christ. If we are the Church, we shouldn't worry that, say, the Vatican and the hierarchy are rigid and unrealistic. That's almost always been the case. The Church doesn't fail when our leaders, who were silent about the destruction of Asian life, grow suddenly outspoken about the destruction of the unborn in our country. It's true that there is an inconsistency there, but we shouldn't have all that much time to notice it.

No, the Church fails when I turn away from my door someone hungry, or in need of a bed. The Church fails when I refuse to listen to a boring woman who wants to analyze the relationship between the Catholic Worker and the history of Women's Rights in the United States. The Church fails at nearly all those times I consider my time my own.

So what should we do about institutional insensitivity and foolishness, about Snoopy-balloon-dancing-bear liturgies, and about tedious debates too shallow to be dignified as heresies? Ignore them, I guess. And silently take Christ as our example.

The amount of attention I pay to my annoyance about the excesses of the new and the timidity of the old Church helps measure my unwillingness to take up the cross.

The vision of Christ's presence leaves little time for anything not centered in the manger, the cross, and the empty tomb. We shouldn't have time for dialogues. Our hands, lives, and time should be full.

It hasn't always been like this.

Once I lived in Davenport, Iowa. I spent lots of time, most of the time, in fact, in the kitchen. During the winter, the poorly insulated house was freezing. We'd turn up the heat full blast, and even then had to wear sweaters and extra socks. During the summer, the poorly-ventilated house was stifling. We'd point malfunctioning fans in every direction—so many of them that fuses would blow, and even then had to wear T-shirts and go barefoot. In every season the house smelled terrible. At dawn, it would smell like socks, socks that hadn't been changed for weeks; by 8:00, it would smell like Pine Sol, socks, sweat, garlic, cigarette smoke, and old onions; by noon, the smell of urine would be added; by five, stale wine and stewing tomatoes; by ten, the smell of socks would have triumphed for the night; and then at dawn, the cycle would repeat itself.

And the noise! Freight trains would shake the foundations (the house is over a railroad track, understand) and the sound of loosening phlegm would gag you.

It was often disgusting, but I could take it, in those days. Young people now aren't as tough as they once were, I'm afraid. I remember the day I went down to the shower stall in the basement to assist Dan Ryan in removing a poisoned rat. The basement looked like the aftermath of some monstrous experiment involving rabid squirrels, a papershredder, tequila and cottage cheese. Awful.

But it's different now. It's a pity I'm on vacation; I'd like to show you how we operate now. I can, however, give you some notion.

Do you see that bank of television screens there? No, there, above that Florentine bookcase. Yes, Dickens' first editions, looted from a Georgia plantation by Sherman's men, I think, but the television screens . . . look. Okay, each one of those receives an image of each room and all sides of West Fifth Street. Only a thirty second delay; it has to bounce off the satellite, and then be transmitted up here from Milan. A little like cable television in the states, I guess. Then there's this microphone on the desk, through which I give orders and encouragement. Of course it works. This is, after all, the land of Marconi!

And then, over there, under the window . . . thank you, Sophia, I'm delighted you like it. I had them landscape it as closely as possible to that Giotto painting of St. Francis meeting the beggar. Oh, I know it sounds a little Southern Californian decadent, but what the hell . . . under the window, that tape recorder plays Burgess Meredith reading Peter Maurin's *Easy Essays* with a thick French accent. While I'm directing stuff at the house, I like to have that in the backgrouund . . . atmosphere, or something. As if you needed atmosphere around here. That sea. Those mountains.

But I'm getting bored with talking about my service for the poor. Let's go for a walk in the garden. I just want to look into your eyes awhile. A man could drown in eyes like yours, Sophia.

What do you mean, the door? It's your imagination; we're alone here, you and I. No one could be knocking at the door.

Someone is.

Pete Domino is.

Yeah, Pete. Do I ever wake you up when you're sleeping? Whattaya mean, soup? Lemme brush my teeth; I'll be over in a minute.

Soup.

Will it always be like this?

I remember a great descriptive reflection by Saul Bellow. In *Mr. Sammler's Planet,* Artur Sammler sits on a Central Park bench watching a panorama of American phenomena:

> Younger people, autochthonous-looking, were also here. Bare feet, the boys like Bombay beggars, beards clotted, breathing rich hair from their nostrils, heads coming through woolen ponchos, somewhat Peruvian. Natives of somewhere. Innocent, devoid of aggression, opting out, much like Ferdinand the Bull.

Dorothy Day, someone told me once, calls them "squatters." They read the *Whole Earth Catalogue,* smoke lots of grass, and eat figs and sunflower seeds. They're into "organic cookery," whatever that is—it is certainly not McDonald's Big Macs, not Hostess Twinkies, not Coca Cola, not, for that matter, my soup, which is often made with a meat base. To the most insignificant statements, they're likely to append, variously, "really," "for sure," and "unreal," each time endowing something banal with an undeserved mystical dimension.

I don't think I like them.

I do like the Grateful Dead, though, and so do most of them. That's what we talk about when I'm trying to be civil with them, trying to work musical small talk around to the subject of when they're getting jobs, when they're moving out or moving on. It's annoying to be forced to turn away unsheltered winos because some bored Larchmont adolescent is hitting the missions and finding himself.

"What you are doing here is really beautiful," one earthwoman told me this morning as I missed a graceful transition from the superb rhythm guitar work of Bob Weir to the fact that she and her boyfriend had hung around for a week with no signs of willingness to leave.

Well, thank you. Under the influence of enough cannabis, everything, from the gurgling of a stopped-up toilet to the shining of the Northern Lights, is "really beautiful." So was her boyfriend, I guess, the swarthy, angry-looking guy with the tattoo on his right forearm which reads, "I'm bound to go to heaven 'cause I spent my time in hell. Danang." So was Jake, the watchdog next door. So was the chipped picnic table in the backyard, where the earthwoman and I sat and talked as her boyfriend glared at both of us from his seat on Pepper's grave.

I was becoming nervous. I was afraid the earthwoman might claim loudly that I myself was beautiful, and that the guy who'd already been in hell would become jealous enough to leap across the backyard and disembowel me as she looked on and pronounced it all "unreal." As Earthwoman continued her discourse on beauty, I felt threatened and lightly equipped, like a paratrooper miles behind enemy lines. The guy who'd already been in hell scratched his tattoo.

"Well anyway, you've had five days and more here, there's a new family coming, you and your friend haven't been doing too much for the past week, and we need the extra space, so you'll have to hit the bricks by tonight, okay?" I'd given up on the Grateful Dead.

Earthwoman parried with the guilt trip: Jesus Christ, what a bummer; here we all were pretending to be Christian and sharing, and all the time we were just as much assholes as all the other bullshit people, etc. (To be called a "bullshit person," by the way, is to be equated with Henry Kissinger, Sammy Davis Jr., Johnny Carson, Nelson Rockefeller, and people like that. It really did sting a little.) But in one way it was a relief to be denounced. The guy who'd had already been in hell relaxed over Pepper's grave, apparently satisfied that Earthwoman would never think me beautiful. He grinned as she continued to accuse, angrily assuring me that Woodstock Nation would leave after lunch.

Later, as I was ladling out soup to the departing earthfolk, and whistling "Casey Jones," Earthwoman said wistfully, "When somebody's whistling, it means they're happy."

No idea what she meant by that; just passing it on.

He's at it again.

He's been at it since four o'clock this morning, and he'll continue for twenty hours, pausing only for meals of peanut butter, toast, tuna fish and coffee . . . and to pee in the Folger's coffee can he keeps on the radiator.

For the next twenty hours there will be four taps of a hammer on the linoleum floor every thirty seconds. Every five minutes there will be an outraged soprano, "You little shit! Go lay down."

Last night I dreamt of railroads.

Railroads we will always have with us—Rock Island Lines, Canadian Pacifics, Illinois Centrals, Grand Trunks, Santa Fes, Royal American Shows, long freights with three loud engines, coal cars, tank cars, cattle cars, refrigerated cars, boxcars with hobo signatures scrawled in yellow chalk on their doors, boxcars disgorging hobos on Fifth Street in front of our house.

Hobos we will always have with us, too. Hobos who draw chalk pictures on boxcars; pictures of gauchos sleeping under palm trees, of curlyheaded nude women, of crosseyed cowboys above the inscription, "Bozo Texino." Hobos with names like Des Moines Red, River Rat, Beefsteak Charlie, Cowboy Bob, Hardrock, and Goatman.

Pete Domino we will, I'm afraid, always have with us, and he's at it again, hammering at the labyrinthine track system which covers most of the floor of his room at Peter Maurin House, screaming at his roommate Kitty Kat for upsetting his Tyco-scale Canadian Pacific.

Pete, his electric trains, and Kitty Kat came with the house, which we got (we thought at the time, before we'd become better acquainted with Pete) for a song. It would have been condemned and demolished if it weren't for the fact that it's a historical landmark, older even than Pete, who is eighty-four and will probably live longer than I. He thrives in this atmosphere, since model railroading is his life-principle.

It's also his emotive medium.

Pete rarely expresses any emotion but clean, obvious hostility, and is most comfortable in a confrontive situation. In fact, he once tried to brain Mother Teresa of Calcutta.

She visited here on a speaking tour of the States and unfortunately attempted to embrace the old guy as he was entering the men's house to yell at anyone handy that he'd run out of whole wheat bread. Pete had never seen a nun in full habit before, and must have assumed that Mother Teresa was handy enough. The holy woman came at him smiling.

"Allo. I em Mudda Treesa from Eendia. Em plees to mit you."

"Get away! Leave me alone! I'm outta bread, goddammit! Where's Margaret? Leave me alone, or I'll slap the shit outtaya!"

The foresight of an alert wino saved the saintly woman from skull fracture. Three-Finger Floyd wrested Pete's cane from the old man's fist before he'd found room to swing it, somebody quickly got Pete a loaf of whole wheat bread, dinner was served, Pete returned to Peter Maurin House triumphantly goddamming everything in sight, and the incident was forgotten.

But it's Pete's more benevolent side that employs model railroading as an emotive medium, and he does, after all, have a benevolent side. Once he invited me into his room to look at back issues of *Model Railroader;* he was, I think, trying to make friends with me after I'd threatened to castrate him for flushing the toilet (into which I imagine he was dumping the contents of his Folger's coffee can) while I was taking a shower, nearly scalding me to death in the process.

I admit that the threat was excessive, and in order to convince him that I had no intention of carrying it out, I entered his room peaceably, careful not to step on his new track, feigning affection for Kitty Kat and interest in model trains.

The meeting was successful. Pete was soon yelling that I was just flipping the pages instead of looking at them, and our comfortable, confrontive, hostile relationship was reestablished.

It's true, though. I wasn't looking at *Model Railroader.* I had become fascinated by other aspects of Pete's room. Beside the door, where a pious Russian would have had an icon, Pete had a reproduction of Veronica's veil. The only other decorations in the room were two color photographs of Pete Domino, and one of Kitty Kat. Beside the mirror over Pete's dresser (the drawers of which were labeled "Rock Island," "GM&O," "CP," and "Grand Trunk"), he'd tacked an index card with the word "taxidermist" and a phone number printed on it. A little alarmed that Pete might be giving up modelrailroading for a new hobby, and one that could jeopardize the maintenance and sanitation of his already filthy room, I asked him about it.

As soon as Kitty Kat dies, Pete explained, he intends to call that number and arrange to have Kitty Kat stuffed and mounted.

He's a complex man.

The Charismaniacs are coming.

I know I'm not openminded. They are good people, even if they are a little intense; they pray fervently for people like me, meeting our defensive cynicism with compassionate, almost aggressive enthusiasm. And if I were maimed and bleeding, hopeless and hostile, they would come to heal me. Christ's apostles at the first Pentecost probably appeared no less silly and threatening . . . or did they? (The exciting thing about the first Pentecost wasn't that nobody could understand what anybody else was saying. It was exciting clarity and not exciting chaos.) It could be that I misunderstand them, that they are trying to make the Good News more rather than less available, that they've experienced the Gospel directly enough to burn away the conventional sorts of behavior that mean so much to inhibited folks like me.

Even so, if I were lying on my deathbed, frightened of the yawning abyss and confronted with armies of taunting, boring, flabby sins; if I realized for the last time that Christ died for us vain and foolish people as well as for the wounded, exploited and abused; if I'd become suddenly aware that I needed all the prayers and support of the Mystical Body to save me, I'd still rather the Charismaniacs weren't there. I'd prefer to have a nervous, shaky, chain-smoking alcoholic priest recently returned from Via Coeli who thinks that they (priests) are professionals and that we (laypeople) are amateurs. He'd have taken to drink out of a vague bitterness he felt in the wake of liturgical change. He'd have found himself unsuited for the public relations work which seemed to him to have overwhelmed the experience of a priestly vocation in today's ministry. He'd be worried that we were losing touch with the two thousand year family history we've accumulated. . . . If he's not around, okay, I'd like them to pray over me, but I'd like at least one of them to be "a duly authorized priest."

Nevertheless, they're coming, and I'm working myself into a bad mood because I know they'll look like Moonies with their wolfish and penetrating eyes, and they'll be enthusiastic. They'll be earnest. They'll be nice people.

They want to start a house. At least, that's what the leader of the group told me about a week ago on the phone. He said that they wanted to come down to Davenport "to see how a Worker house operates," and I'd said sure. All fourteen of them.

I should have known better. There are few things more insulting and awkward for the guys than to be put on display, like zoo animals for tourists. ("And these are the poor winos we work with, folks.") And now I have visions of leading fourteen people through the dorm rooms, stepping around Harry Allen's coffee cans, past Todd West rocking and giggling in his chair, over Tim Marley in full lotus position contemplating a photograph of his estranged wife. Why did I say sure?

Because I wasn't thinking clearly at the time. I was preoccupied. More precisely, I was putting three tablespoons of sugar into Harry Allen's vegetable soup. I would have let the old guy do it himself, but he would have put a cup in, and sugar is expensive, and three tablespoons are probably bad enough for the old guy. God only knows what else he eats during the day.

I should have said no. I should have said that two or three could come. We should start saying no to everyone who wants to come and look, even with the finest intentions . . . but it's too late.

They're here. They come charging in like a chapter from a Eudora Welty novel—an aging hippie with hornrim glasses and a pipe, swinging two noisy little girls at his sides; an angry looking middle-aged woman with closely cropped hair; three? four? bony teenaged girls; a few bald young men (refugees from the Alabama-Freedom-Riders-Peter-Paul-and-Mary era, maybe), and I can't even see the rest of them as the screen door continues to bang and the kitchen begins to fill. The guys from the house are retreating in all directions. Larry, with whom I'd been arguing about how to spell "cognizance" in his crossword puzzle (he'd said no "z"), has vanished, leaving me alone with the visitors. I'll kill him.

There we all are, standing in the kitchen of the

Catholic Worker House, looking as funky and various as a group portrait of the Grateful Dead, they, smiling and blinking, I, wondering what the hell to tell them, worrying that they might try to evangelize some of the guys or, even worse, me. There are introductions (I can remember Ralph the Hippie, Steve the Bald, and Mary the Angry) and it's time for the tour to begin. I wish Margaret would come in. Or John. Or anyone who could talk long enough for me to sneak away.

Well, this is the kitchen, of course. This is the dining room (there is complete silence in the house, suddenly, except for the shuffling of fifteen pairs of shoes and my lecture). This is where the guys sleep, and we can fit six more guys on the floor in the dining room and the living room. These are the johns, and then there's a shower stall in the basement. This is Old Harry Allen (looking at all of us as if we were a herd of buffalo passing his bed). Hi, Harry. This is the back kitchen. (Margaret! John! Someone! Please!) We sleep upstairs, well, actually no, I sleep over at Peter Maurin House. So does. . . . There are five of us. No, six. No, seven. It's kind of strange. (Is it ever just.)

The Hippie: You take in everybody?

CW: As long as they're relatively sober and can't afford a room someplace else. We used to let everyone in, and it just got too crazy. Fights,

broken windows, chaos, and all that bullshit
(oops—Mary the Angry looks angrier). Oh, and
they have to be . . . well, we close the door at ten
. . . and if we ever have more than about eigh-
teen guys we . . . .

Mary the Angry: Do you ever have to ask people
to leave?

CW: Well, if a guy's violent, or brings a bottle of
booze into the house, or just. . . .

Mary the Angry: Sometimes, you just have to
realize that the most loving thing to do is harsh, is
that it?

CW: Yeah, that's really true.

No, that's not really true. John and Margaret have
come back, and are doing a much better job than I.
I've escaped. I am in hiding at Peter Maurin House,
listening to Pete's hammer as he reroutes his Canadian Pacific Line to make room for his new roundhouse. It's not true, or at least it's not true that I kick
people out for loving reasons. That freaky Chicano
kid who clocked Aloysius, he scares me and I hate
him. Carrack, stumbling around with a load in his
pants and whining to everyone . . . I don't want to
be near him when he's like that. Oswald, being ob-
sequious as he drunkenly spills soup all over the
place. Tommy ranting about hydrogen bombs and

biblical portents . . . we tell ourselves and each other (at least, I tell myself) that it's for the community's peace we give them the boot. It might be partly true.

But the relief I feel when they're out of my sight, when they leave with all their torments raging, their suffering unattended, their whole personalities rejected and wretched, that relief condemns me. It's the pattern of the crucifixion all over again, and it's certainly not me on the cross. There's no solace in telling ourselves that loving acceptance of those we find most repulsive is work for the saints alone, because that's a lie. In our own twisted ways, in our own trivial, selfish, halfhearted ways, haven't we tried to make life on Davenport's skid row a little more merciful? Isn't that enough? Obviously not.

Damn those Charismaniacs.

Jack jumped a Kansas City-bound freight last night. It was an event.

I was upstairs looking at a map of Iowa when I heard the whistle of the west-bound engine, which was probably then crossing the Mississippi at the government bridge. I'd remembered seeing Jack sitting on the curb in front of the house a few hours before, mildly stoned and saying over and over again, I'm goinhometiddee yeslordgoinhometidee. He'd apparently told everyone at the house the same thing, since there was a crowd gathered at the steps of the porch to watch the attempt.

One veteran of the rails watched the oncoming white and blue engine (there were four of them, indicating at least a hundred cars would follow; this meant that Jack would be able to pick and choose) and shook his head. "Little too fast, I'd say."

Three or four hobos stood at the corner to the left of the porch, muttering together like professional athletes watching a promising rookie's technique. Jack had stationed himself about half a block down the street, facing west and crouched like a sprinter, right foot braced against a fire hydrant.

Ten cars passed, not including the four engines. I started to worry a little. I've never jumped a freight, but it seemed to me that the train was going pretty fast, and Jack was, after all, loaded enough to take a stupid risk. I had watched a drunk jump a freight much slower than this one, only seconds after I'd kicked him out of the house one Fall afternoon, and he barely made it, even though he was not as drunk as Jack.

Jack started to rock back on his right foot after ten more cars, and then started his sprint. It seemed that the train was going about five miles an hour faster than Jack by the time he reached the corner. He jumped, getting his left foot on the lowest rung, and his left hand, with what looked like a pretty decent grip, about four rungs higher up. His target had been the ladder at the front of a coal car. There was one gut-wrenching moment when his right leg dipped dangerously close to the big wheels, but by the time the coal car drew abreast of the front porch, Jack was steady, grinning and waving to our applause and shouted goodbyes. "I'll check ya'all out when I'm through this way again!" It was a glorious moment.

A few of the hobos seemed a little envious of Jack's skillful jump. This inexperienced turkey had outdone them, had outdone even their exaggerated stories about different jumps they'd made in the past, and all in one impulsive, graceful moment. Jack had, by the time the coal car was out of sight, made it up the ladder and onto the heap of coal above.

Al was a little huffy. "Dumb nigger," he muttered, "coulda got hisself killed jumpin' somethin' that fast." And then, as the train slowed for the curve about a mile west of the house, ". . . and look there, coulda got hisself a boxcar if he'd been more patient."

I couldn't resist. "Face it, Al boy. You've just been outclassed." I don't know what I expected as a result, but I did get a very dark look. Al outweighs me by about forty pounds and is easily a foot taller, so I softened it. "Wouldn't that burn his ass if it was headed for Winnipeg?" Al laughed, and followed me inside to tell me about the time he'd dropped ten feet from a viaduct onto a load of gravel. It was probably a lie, but it was a great story. By the time he'd finished it, his freight train had been going sixty miles an hour. Jack's, I suppose, was crossing Iowa cornfields on its way home.

There is one tension at this place that is probably more important than any other. It's between the plight of the staff and the plight of our guests. It's irreconcilable.

We've chosen to be here, and that's a luxury of the class, culture, economic system (or whatever it is) into which we were born. At any moment, we know, we could leave West Fifth Street for a clean, air conditioned place where we would be welcomed and loved.

They can't. They are "disadvantaged," which is what we say when we mean weak, wretched, outcast, and despised. Three-quarters of the people who come through our door every day would be "disadvantaged" in 13th century Europe, 20th century China, the America of the 1930s . . . in any society that anyone can imagine.

We wouldn't. We have a certain level of education, a certain connection with the wealthy and powerful, maybe even a certain willingness to compromise and lie, which would enable us to be comfortable and safe in this or any other system. For all of our attempts to identify with the poor and the weak, we will never share with them the involuntary nature of their poverty.

But there are, nevertheless, moments when the distinction between a staff member and a guest breaks down, when a volunteer is forced to realize that he or she is as broken and wretched as a conscript. Probably everyone associated with the Catholic Worker could tell of such moments. They're difficult to articulate, which is probably why they're seldom related.

Somewhere in the Quad Cities Area (I hope, at the moment, in jail) there is a crazy, mean Chicano kid about twenty years old. He appears at the house sporadically, like an inexplicable bad mood. I once knew what his name is, but I've forgotten it for some vague emotional reason.

I hate his guts.

He stayed with us here at the house the first few days I did. He was your basic North American hippie, rootless and goofy; he'd hitchhiked up here from the Southwest for no real reason, winding up out of money, out of work, out of anything to do, out of his mind, at our house.

One night, he stumbled into dinner, tequila-crazed and violent, yelling about how much he hated niggers, how he'd been fucked over by hillbillies and Anglos, how he wanted to kill himself a nigger. We kicked him out. Dinner time can be unpleasant enough without all that. I think I was starting to hate him then. He managed to get in again, through the back door, I guess, and to beat up old Aloysius Grant, a gentle, slightly mad black man.

Louie, another guest, an alcoholic ex-minister, helped us shove the screaming kid out the front door, down the steps and into the street while John took care of Aloysius. Louie's was the Christian response: "Just let's talk to him a minute; he'll cool off." Mine wasn't, and still isn't. I asked Louie to tell that fucking asshole never to come back here again; I was in the teeth of the same hatred that impelled the kid to beat up Aloysius.

I realized, when our hating eyes met on the street that the only thing that distinguished us from each other was that my address was 806 West Fifth Street.

He had no address, then or now.

Mike:

> Loretta called and would like you to check the room where Jane and Betty are staying around midnight. Apparently Jane burns a candle and papers on the floor of the room & Betty is scared & Loretta worried. I know this sounds crazy but it's the best I can explain it. Thanks.
>
> Bert

Was I losing my grip? Had I been on the job too long? Bert's note made perfect sense to me. The reason St. Jane was burning a candle and papers (small, strategically placed fires on the linoleum floor of her room at Peter Maurin House) was to ward off the devils that float around here.

She had told me this, and many other things during the brief time that I knew her. She had admitted me to her confidence because I was, in her strange way of looking at the world, the only person around here, other than she herself, who was not possessed.

The truck parked in front of Peter Maurin House was a black and white devil. Loretta drove the truck, and brought devils into the house with her, even though she didn't mean to. St. Jane was understanding and tolerant within her circle of candles and fires.

But we had to ask her not to build fires on the floor of this highly flammable building, and she became afraid that we'd been swayed by devils and unwittingly included in their conspiracy against her. St. Jane decided that she was no longer welcome here and left as oddly as she arrived.

She arrived on a 90-degree day with a winter coat on. She had a red Samsonite suitcase and four large boxes with "Do not touch my property" written on each. There was a pink bath towel wrapped turban-like around her head, fastened with what looked like a turquoise belt buckle. A pretty, middle-aged black lady, all smiles, and with a lovely singsong voice she introduced herself, enunciating all her words like a third grader in Reading Class. "How do you do? I am St. Jane, from Chicago, Illinois. I'm not crazy, thank the Lord, and I thank you very dearly for inviting me to share your home, since I am temporarily in need of shelter, as you know. Who am I talking to, please? How do you do, God bless you. Many men seem afraid of the name Michael, thinking that it sounds effeminate, but after all, the Holy Spirit made him the chief of all the archangels, as you know, so that is very unnecessary. These are my things, do be careful with them, please, and God will reward you, I'm sure, for your great kindness."

That was far from the end of her speech, but it's all I can remember. St. Jane was a delightful person, even if she was nuts, and even if the four boxes were heavy. As we struggled with them up the winding staircase of Peter Maurin House, St. Jane smiled, laughed, and rejoiced that the Holy Spirit had shown her to this new place. She settled in as I tried to soothe Pete, who was already screaming about another damn nigger in the house. ("Pete, don't use that word in front of me, or I'll break you over my knee. I mean it, now.")

"Oh, shit. Everybody says not to call 'em niggers, but goddamit, Mike, they ain't Chinamen!" I gave up.

Jane cheerfully endured Pete, and seemed happy for a while.

Then the devils came.

Loretta's devil explained that there would be a family of five coming within the next five days, by which time St. Jane would have to make other arrangements for a place to stay. Loretta's devil was even willing to help her get in touch with social workers, welfare programs, Salvation Army people, or anyone else. St. Jane began to kindle her fires.

Dawn Russo's devil insisted that she not kindle fires on the floor of Peter Maurin House. St. Jane hissed that Dawn had gone over to their side. The gentle suggestion that St. Jane should perhaps think about seeing a doctor was too much, and the poor crazy lady asked me if I would be so kind as to drive her back to Rock Island. I had welcomed her into my home, while the others had unfortunately listened to the devils who opposed her. There were no hard feelings because it wasn't our fault—it was just that the devils had found her through us, rather, through the others, because she was sure that I was not their agent.

We had to take the black and white truck, which was by now, apparently, exhausted of devils. We loaded it with her suitcase and boxes (on which she had changed the inscriptions to "Thou shalt not steal") and drove across the Centennial Bridge to Illinois.

St. Jane, on the way over, told me that she intended to return to Chicago: I asked her what she would do when she returned. She would do what the Spirit commanded. Would she call us if there was anything we could do? If she had trouble with a bus ticket, for instance? That wouldn't be necessary, she said, because God and the Holy Spirit and Jesus, our Lord and Savior were always with her, and she was more concerned with the Father's glory than with her own comfort. I believe that.

If I would only be so kind as to drive her to the steps of the YWCA, which was a Christian organization, as I no doubt knew, that would be more than sufficient.

St. Jane smiled benevolently as I unloaded the truck, stacking her boxes and suitcase around her on the steps of the YWCA. She stood on the highest step, both hands plunged into the pockets of her thick coat.

"Goodbye, Michael. Will you do me a favor? This Pentecost, put on a suit and tie instead of those old clothes. Not for my honor, but for the honor of the Holy Spirit. God bless you."

That was the last I saw of St. Jane. She apparently visited two or three churches in Rock Island, and got on the bus for Chicago.

I couldn't find a suit this Pentecost.

Soup.

One of the by-products of involvement with the Catholic Worker movement is a deeper enjoyment of soup. It would not be reckless to say that the soupline at noon on Fifth Street has introduced many hungry people to a culinary experience that would make Julia Child, the Galloping Gourmet, the kitchen staffs of Le Perroquet and Le Pavillon all hang their heads in shame. There is no secret recipe for Catholic Worker Soup; the unstructured and arbitrary methods by which it is produced have, at times, resulted in disappointments, but are more often striking examples of the poetry engendered when the undisciplined imagination confronts kitchen hardware and barren icebox.

The hardware problem is easy; a large pot, a long spoon, and a sharp knife. That elegantly simple trinity, if your goal is good, honest soup, is all you need.

Some things to be kept in mind:

1. In the early days of the Catholic Worker, Peter Maurin and Dorothy Day thought that it would be a good idea to keep a soup pot simmering at all times. This could be continually replenished by whatever vegetables the people of the house could acquire. It was a brilliant idea for a symbol of communal sharing, certainly. But, even more certainly, it was responsible for delicious soup. The longer soup simmers, obviously, the better it tastes, and the

vegetables and flavors that do not become compatible, even complementary, after four hours companionship in a boiling pot are rare.

2. Far too many modern problems (our fascination with violence, our racism, our waste of resources, our fragmentation as people) are grounded in unnecessary fears. One minor, but definitely unnecessary fear is the fear of making too much soup. Soup that has been reheated after forty-eight hours in the refrigerator tastes much better than the soup you made this morning, and serves as an excellent theme for even better soup. I like to think that in the soup I had at noon today, there may have been a few dim atoms of the soup served on the day our house here opened. Good soup is one more way we can preserve the treasures of the past, and demonstrates that tradition is never a dead thing, but always a fresh and enriching perspective on the present. Good soup has, in common with great art, and the Gospel itself, the characteristic of eternal freshness and beauty.

3. The phrase "too much garlic" is meaningless.

4. So is the phrase "too many onions."

5. The idea may be unorthodox, but sometimes, by concentration on visual aesthetics, to the exclusion of the more vulgar urgings of the palate, one can stumble into higher realms of soup-making and

soup-eating pleasure. About a month ago, I emptied an annoying can of catsup (it had wasted space in our icebox for too long and its moment had come) into what had previously been an uninteresting liquid of drab, brown appearance. I stirred in the catsup hesitantly, watching deep red clouds from the bottom of the soup kettle merge gently with the brown. Soon the pot was simmering again, this time with a wine-dark surface. It smelled wonderful, but tasted strangely sweet. Onion salt, gradually added, brought the taste of the soup from sweet to rich. More space in the icebox. Better looking soup. Better tasting soup (the men in the house nearly all came back for seconds) and a proud and happy soupmaker. All of this as a result of inclusion rather than exclusion.

It wouldn't hurt to remember that soup is best as a shared food; that all food becomes better when shared. This is what the miracle of loaves and fishes teaches us. This is what the child's story "Nail Broth" celebrates. Most people on the North American continent have at this moment, in their refrigerators, ingredients which, when added to a quart or so of boiling water, could delight and enrich them. Especially if they used too much of everything, and invited too many to eat with them. The reason that such an idea is preposterous to us is our own unnecessary fear.

Catholic Worker contra mundum: a telephone dialogue.

"Hello. Catholic Worker House."

"Right. This is Marge from PGUPD."

"PGUPD?"

"Right. What are your income guidelines?"

"Income guidelines?"

"Right. We have a TMNVMS who needs a thrax-engrant but HFS can't at the moment come across with the NPG, since he falls outside their income guidelines. What are yours?"

"Did you say your name was Marge?"

"Right."

"Right. Marge, I haven't had a cup of coffee yet, so I'm probably not understanding real well. Could you run this whole thing by me again?"

"Is this the Catholic Worker House?"

"Right, Marge."

"You're the agency that provides EA's to TMNVMS exigencies, right? You do have income guidelines, don't you?"

"Marge?"

"Right."

"I don't think I know what an income guideline is. No, we're not an agency."

"But don't you provide EA to TMNVMS exigencies? HFS gave me your number."

"Marge?"

"Right."

"Do you have a guy there?"

"Right. Transient male, 36; gave your address there as his most recent BVF; he's applying for NPG, but he falls outside their income guidelines. Look, all I want to know is whether or not your agency has BVG cutoff points."

"Beats me, frankly. What's the guy's name?"

"Watts, Martin. His GHY doesn't scan with our FRP."

"Marge?"

"Right."

"Can you put him on the phone?"

"No."

"How come?"

"Our IGP standard for . . ."

"Okay, can you describe him then?"

"Well, tall, blue eyes, tattoo on . . ."

"Hold it, Marge. Is that him yelling in the background?"

"Right."

"I might know who it is. Does he answer to the name of River Rat, or just River?"

"Just a minute. Right."

"How loaded is he? Pretty bad?"

"Well . . ."

"Just a little weavy, right?"

"Right."

"Marge, just tell him he's not getting anywhere with TVA, or whatever it is, and tell him we said that his thirty days are up. Tell him to come on down for a bowl of soup, and if he's sober enough by ten, we'll even get him a bed. How'd that be?"

"Right. Just super. See, we'd get him an NPG, but he . . ."

"Let me guess . . . your income guidelines?"

"Oh no, not ours. See, HFS has. . . ."

"Oh, yeah, I'd forgotten that. Okeydoke, Marge."

"Right. Bye now."

If you're not yet inured to metropolitan phenomena, West Madison Street in Chicago, as much as any street in a large city, reminds you of a Donald Duck comic book. Against the urban background you see a cartoonlike procession of figures and faces. There's something predominantly humanoid about them, but their number and variety generate traces of moose, bear, lizard, horse, and squirrel. Ears start to look funny; clothes start to look like scales, fur, or plumage. As in any big city, you start to feel like a Martian observing earthfolk for the first time.

Madison Street West can be distinguished from most other streets by the absence, even the impossibility, of comedy in that grotesque and variegated flow. Many of the faces grin or contort with laughter, but in the expression there's always something mirthless and loony, something threatening. There's no room for joy in this craziness.

Because this is a part of Chicago's skid row, and almost everyone you meet here is drunk. Not happy, charming, roguish, celebratory drunk, either. Here people from all over the continent gather together, not because they want to be together, but because West Madison Street is for them a place of refuge. Here they can, in relative safety and peace, consume enough white port to deaden a pain that no one has yet named.

All the cliches about the loneliness of big cities, about the lost, lonely, broken souls in the middle of the crowd here take on a new and deeper intensity. This is the end of the road for a lonely person and there is no possibility here for a romantic, or hopeful, or even benevolently poignant ending. Folks here are entrenched in their loneliness; armed with gallons of wine, they're making a last stand against the something awful that has pursued them to this place.

It's hard to tell where these people live. Or survive. Most of the buildings are deserted and seem uninhabitable. There are a few obvious flops (one of which is the Star Hotel, where Richard Speck slept before committing mass murder), but most West Madison Street residents sleep, literally, on the street, on benches and sidewalks, in gutters and doorways and alleys. Most of them are men.

When I was there I saw only one woman.

She was about my mother's age, I think, but it was hard to tell. Alcohol and streetlife seemed to have made her age an insignificant riddle buried under years and years of suffering. She was sitting on the only fragment of vegetable life for miles around, an overgrown island in the middle of a bulldozed lot. Surrounded by discarded beer cans and broken pint bottles, she was puffing a handrolled cigarette and watching the back of a retreating wino with whom she'd apparently just finished an argument. Her head was rocking strangely from side to side and she was screaming something incoherent through a gruesome smile. He ignored her, crossing the street and narrowly missing the wheels of an eastbound city bus. It seemed that already the screech of the tires, her insults and their quarrel were equally ancient experiences for him. He looked like he needed a drink.

Many of the guys at our house have done time on West Madison Street. Frypan Tim, a reputable hobo, even claims to have stayed at the Star Hotel, which he described as "a filthy, stinking hole of a place." And Frypan Tim has, I'm sure, stayed in some pretty raunchy places. What all the guys seem to agree on is that West Madison Street is rough. Street violence is frequent, probably because there aren't enough "citizens" in the area to make panhandling profitable. I noticed only one day-labor place, which I'm sure couldn't have accommodated the thousands of men on the street that day.

But there has to be enough collective income, and enough inhuman retailing to keep West Madison Street fueled with booze. It's a paradox of the culture that a smack dealer's immeasurable cruelty and exploitation puts him outside the law, while a liquor retailer on West Madison Street pays his taxes, has the vote, and enjoys the protection of the judicial system as he makes money on equally broken souls.

The place is a desert. It's the sort of place which almost audibly cries out for the presence of Christ, or for the recognition and reverencing of that presence; it's the sort of place which draws Christ.

It's a perfect place for a Catholic Worker house. Someone should open one there. I couldn't take it. In comparison, the poverty and suffering that we see here have a mild and pastoral quality. I'll settle for that, and leave the West Madison Streets and Calcuttas of this world for the saints.

Anality explains why men yearn for freedom
from contradictions and ambiguities, why they
like their symbols pure, their truth with a capital
"T."

Ernst Becker, *The Denial of Death*

Undoubtedly. But all I ask, after having been delivered from this clotted, messy, incomplete universe, is a bathroom that smells more like Pine Sol
than like Pete's feces.

Ours is, I'm afraid, a classically anal household.
We long to be released from contradictions and ambiguities all right, and it should by now be obvious
that we're engulfed by them, but that's still not the
true source of our compulsion. We have, after all,
the Gospel, the promise of a new life, of a new and
finer order which, if it doesn't diminish our fear of
death, at least places the inevitability of death in a
timeless pattern we can accept. That's not the problem.

Because, for instance, there's nothing particularly
ambiguous about Old Harry's failure to achieve his
morning evacuation. That's implacable.

Symbols, myths, souls, life principles, unnamed
fears, all these can do what they like. There remains
an intrinsic relationship between the motion of
Harry's bowels and the enterprise of hospitality.
More precisely, when Old Harry has a hard time on

the stool, we all have a hard time getting through the day.

One time we (I mean the staff, guests, and Harry's large intestine) were paralyzed for forty-eight hours.

Old Harry is usually the first man awake in the house. At least the first man audibly awake. If you were to pass his bed at three in the morning in your stocking feet, he'd be likely to yell, "Great day for a coyote hunt!" "Call me Kid Muleskinner?" "Halfa-bowladynamite?" or something like that.

But one ominously quiet morning he was found sitting upright in bed looking pensive and vulnerable. His voice sounded almost repentant, as if he'd let us all down, as if he were not as sorry for himself as for the whole house:

"Will you tell Margaret my bowels won't move."

In quavery, unconvincing tones we tried to assure him that there'd be no problem at all, that we'd have him running as smoothly as a well-adjusted clock in no time; still, the brevity and solemnity of his reply, that he'd do whatever we told him "to get things goin' all right again" was alarming. Harry knew, as we all did, that this was to be no easy battle.

The guys pitched in. Steve Ames' mother, when he was little, had used chocolate syrup and kerosene (he *thought*, but wasn't sure) on these occasions. Too daring an idea, we decided. I'd read once in a bartender's manual of a drink which combined prune juice, vodka, and soda water. The name came to me, and it was inspiring. The Piledriver.

We decided on a variation. Into a tall glass we poured prune juice, mineral oil, apple juice, and warm water. Harry drained it in three gulps, returned with great difficulty to his bed, and for two hours stared, silent and unblinking, at the bathroom door. Nothing.

At lunchtime, one of the guys asked Harry if he wanted his customary halfabowl.

Harry said: "I'm all plugged up. Can't make it no worse."

"*Egg* yolks! Egg yolks, chocolate syrup, and just a splash of kerosene," said Steve Ames. "I know it sounds weird."

Too weird, Steve.

We had him taking prune juice like oxygen until shortly before dinnertime, when one guy ran into the kitchen, breathless. "The old man's on the john!" We put a dab of margarine into his coffee cup for his victorious dinner, but when old Harry entered a silent dining room, all the guests pretending not to study his face, he looked disappointed. "I couldn't get all of it out, fellas." He didn't want anything to eat. Said he couldn't get away with it.

At a pharmacy we purchased a non-prescription laxative that doubled as a sewer cleaner. Harry drank about half a gallon before going to bed. We were getting worried.

It was an uneasy night. Harry sat up in bed staring at the bathroom door. Upstairs in the community room, we spoke about trying a sudden midnight scare. Sleepless across the aisle from Old Harry's bed, Steve Ames (he told me later) remembered that it wasn't kerosene at all; it was motor oil . . . thirty-weight.

Everyone was up early, spaced-out and grumpy.

"Anything yet, Harry?"

"Nope." We called the doctor, who told us to give what he referred to as "the problem" another twenty-four hours. Then we were to administer one of the disposable enemas he'd left with us.

We started to pray, and also, of course, to draw straws. I won (or lost, depending on how you look at it). The fact that Old Harry weighs at least three hundred pounds and is incapable of moving faster than thirty feet an hour made the notion of giving him an enema triply unattractive.

Tempers were flaring by noon, when, over his twelfth glass of prune juice, Harry said he was interested in a more potent response to "the problem." Together we went over the different remedies we'd tried. I had the enema in my hand.

"Let's give it another couple of hours, Harry. If nothing's happened by then, we'll bring in the artillery." Harry asked what I was holding. I told him, explaining how it worked, how it would hurt me far more than it would hurt him. He looked startled.

"I'll have another go at it," he said. The bathroom door closed.

It was shortly before dinner that the back of the house shook with Old Harry's roar. "Call me Kid Sidewinder!"

I ran into the back yard and heaved the enema as high into the air as I could, for sheer joy. Back to those happy ambiguities. Those blessed contradictions!

Steve Billings sporadically employs himself as a carnival barker. He has the voice for it. As half a dozen of us stood in a semicircle watching an ambulance attendant beam a thin ray of light into Larry's unresponsive iris, Steve explained, in the same piercing voice that had awakened Dawn and me at seven in the morning to call for help, everything he knew.

Which was that Larry and Carrack had been in an argument, that Carrack had been pretty drunk and had taken a swing, that Larry had collapsed on the front porch, and that Carrack had disappeared.

We followed the ambulance to the hospital and watched Larry, the stretcher, the ambulance attendants, and four or five sprinting hospital personnel disappear through the swinging doors of the emergency room.

As we were giving the desk clerk the little information we had about Larry, a priest hurried past us into the emergency room. The desk clerk asked what Larry's religion was. I'd lived with Larry for a year and had only discovered the night before, while we were picking up leftover dinners from a restaurant near the house. We had driven by a Lutheran church and Larry said that a long time ago he had been a Lutheran.

Larry had shown up about a year earlier, still reeling from the effects of some experience too difficult or too painful for him to describe in much detail. He had referred to himself then in the third person, Richard Nixon style . . . "Larry will be all right here. Larry just needs a place to get back on his feet." Gradually, he'd become as "normal" as anyone at our house can become. He'd joined the staff of the place.

After a few minutes, the priest emerged. "You're with Mr. Spiegel?"

"Yes."

"Well, they're doing all they can for him. He's unconscious, but I said a few prayers with him." He didn't seem to know what to say. Neither did we. Suddenly the priest said, "He's a Lutheran, as you know." Dawn was starting to cry.

From the hospital, we went to Mass. It was midmorning by the time we returned to the house. By then, everyone knew that Larry had died. The police had been by, looking for Carrack. One of the guys had fixed Old Harry's oatmeal, which Larry had customarily done. Harry didn't seem to notice any difference.

At noon, Carrack showed up, trembling, sober, and pathetic. He asked if Larry were dead, and then burst into tears. Brennan had run into him in a downtown bar and told him about it. Carrack and Larry had been close friends. He came upstairs with us to wait for the police, who were on their way.

It was not the fight that killed Larry, the postmortem showed, but a heart attack brought on, I suppose, by the rage of the argument that started it. Carrack was back at the house for dinner, hopelessly drunk by now, and still in tears. Norm Brady, a huge and preternaturally shy black man stood up at grace to ask for a special prayer for Larry. A fight started in the back yard.

A new guy started it. I don't remember much about him, except that his name was Billy, and that he was a mean drunk, looking for any excuse to fight. Larry's death had provided him one. "Larry was a great man, and that son of a bitch kills him, and you let that son of a bitch *stay*. You gonna let that motherfucker have Larry's *bed* tonight?" We kicked him out. As he stumbled over the railroad tracks, Billy yelled, "Carrack! Billy gonna make you pay!"

About twenty of the guys from the house went to the funeral, where a whitehaired man told us that the Shepherd's Psalm was like a diadem of beautiful words woven together by strands of love.

Carrack stayed drunk for about a month afterwards, and then left for Chicago.

***The winter of 1976-1977, you remember, was harsh enough to make the cover of* Time *magazine*—competing with a faltering economy, the bicentennial celebration, and the spread of terrorism as a justifiable focus of media analysis. Buffalo, New York, I think, was declared a disaster area. Rumors were spreading about the onslaught of a new Ice Age, and suddenly weathermen became celebrities. Public relations people in Washington were using the weather to advance the new administration's energy program.

Its impact was felt no less by America's transient population. A clumsy hobo in Oregon managed to lock himself into a boxcar, narrowly escaping a frozen death. Both his arms and one leg were amputated. Three Finger Floyd passed out in a lumber yard and froze to death. Freight-hopping slowed down considerably; making out the guest list at the Catholic Worker house became a sort of archaic ceremony, a recopying of the previous night's names. The crowd at dinnertime rarely exceeded thirty, which was a significant decrease from the summer.

Among the very few who continued to ride the rails after the Fall was a lanky, whitehaired New Englander who showed up smashed on muscatel and still shivering one night shortly after dinner. Whoever was taking the list that night overlooked (or oversmelled) the booze on his breath, gave him a chair in the living room, and told him to sleep it off. Such rule-bending is 'pretty rare at the house, even on nasty nights, not only because it's unfair to the guys who are trying to keep sober for a few days, but because it provides ammunition for the uncontrollably belligerent drunk who is asked to leave. But this night, none of the guys complained. There was a blizzard outside and Three Finger's death was horribly fresh in everyone's memory. Also this guy, Todd, seemed to be unusually nice, with his generous, loaded grin and kindly, bloodshot eyes. He was a favorite from the start.

In the morning, as I was slicing onions for the soup, Todd came into the kitchen for a cup of coffee. As far as I knew, no one had yet told him about our rules, but he immediately spoke of his gratitude for the rulebending of the night before. He was thinking about sticking around for a few days, thinking about looking for work here. But from now on he wanted to be treated like everyone else. No playing favorites.

I told him that he shouldn't worry. He'd hate us all in a week. He didn't say anything for awhile.

After he had finished his coffee, he asked if there were anything he could do. My eyes were weeping from the onion-slicing, and I hadn't heard the other side of the Thelonius Monk album that a friend had given me for my birthday, and I was sick of being at the Catholic Worker house, and I wanted to see if

the throbbing in my right big toe was in fact the ingrown toenail I suspected. "Sure," I said. "Why
don't you finish these onions, wash the dishes, and
run a mop over the floor?" I showed him how to
chop onions, which is a little like showing someone
how to use a broom, but Todd listened attentively.

My eyes, after I sat upstairs for half an hour of
Monk, stopped stinging. I was still sick of the
Catholic Worker, and a careful examination had
yielded substantial evidence that an ingrown toenail
was developing on my right big toe. I'd read
somewhere that a son of Calvin Coolidge died as a
result of an infected ingrown toenail. Or maybe it
was a blister on his heel. At any rate, foot trouble,
serious infection, and death were all on my mind as I
limped back into the kitchen. That may be why I felt
a surge of annoyance when I saw that Todd hadn't
finished with the dishes yet. I could be dead in
another week, and this yoyo was making me waste
precious remaining moments of my life with un-
finished onion-slicing by lingering over unwashed
coffee cups. "What about the onions?" I snarled.

"Take a look."

In the soup kettle was simmering a vegetable beef
combination that looked like an advertisement for
the Catholic Worker. Then I realized that the floor
had been scrubbed instead of mopped, as had the
gleaming stove. I realized that he scrubbed the sink,
too. I grunted something like "Hang in there, Todd,"

and headed back upstairs to listen to more piano music. What was this guy's story?

His story was legion, because I can't remember all of it, but here are some highlights: He had been a truckdriver, an ironworker, a deserter from the army, a bartender, a felon and a convict. At least, I assume that he had been a felon, because he'd learned to cook, he said, in jail, where he'd spent three years. He'd destroyed a semi after a forty-eight hour North-South run during which he'd used beer the way less imaginative truckdrivers use dexedrine. He'd run a diner in Lincoln, Nebraska; he'd cooked on an oil rig in the Gulf of Mexico. He had a daughter in Worcester, Massachusetts, whom he hadn't seen for ten years. "I get to drinkin', and I'm too loony for 'em." He spoke of his drinking fondly . . . the old days of yelling and dancing in front of his family's house in Fall River, of singing to the cops from the drunk tank, of seducing a beautiful woman at an AA meeting. He couldn't see how people got in fights when they drank, said Todd, 'cause when he drank, all he wanted to do was laugh and sing and screw. "But there ain't nothin' I can do about that last part; too old," he would always add.

(The times I saw Todd loaded were never so pastoral. He always seemed dazed and broken and sad.)

That night Todd made chicken and dumplings for thirty people. He also baked ten loaves of whole wheat bread. And four apple pies. He rearranged the spice shelf and started to make out a grocery list. After he had scrubbed down the kitchen until it was ready for surgery, he made coffee, drinking from a cup on which he'd written "Cook." Somewhere he found an orange apron, and it became part of his uniform, along with his cowboy boots.

Todd woke up every morning at four o'clock. By six, at which time most of the other guys would be getting up to look for work at the temporary labor pool, three pots of coffee would be brewed, Old Harry would be smacking his lips after his second bowl of prune juice, breadcrumbs, oatmeal and coffee (which Todd always prepared without comment), fresh biscuits would have been baked, and the grocery list would be finished. By the time lunch was served, the main dish for dinner would be cooking in the back kitchen. While we would be upstairs in the community room (watching the television program "Upstairs/Downstairs," and remarking on the similarity of Todd West to Angus Hudson), Todd would be going to bed, preparing for the next cycle. He became a sort of custodian for the house, as well as the cook, recruiting other guys for onion-chopping, dishwashing, floor-scrubbing, bathroom-painting, and snow-shoveling. We found ourselves buying him cigarettes regularly, although he at first objected. ("I ain't no different from these other guys.") Anyone so compulsive about work needed a pack of smokes a day, we figured.

He flourished. When Old Harry needed a shave, it turned out that Todd had been a barber. When the '64 Chrysler broke down, it turned out that Todd had been a mechanic. When the bathroom was unoccupied, but locked, it turned out that Todd had been a locksmith (or it could be that the ease with which he picked the lock was related to the amount of time he'd spent in prison). It was Todd who showed us how to clean glass with newspaper. It was Todd who could translate Jimmy's impeded speech into Massachusetts-accented English. The staff of the Catholic Worker house was becoming happily obsolete.

One day there was a leak in the bathroom sink, and Todd, of course, was the man to fix it. The job grew more and more complex, and before long the bathroom was ankle deep with foul-smelling water and small hardware. He needed a couple of washers; we gave him money for them, and he left. He didn't return that night. By morning it was obvious that we needed more than a couple of washers. We called a plumber, who replaced about a foot of rusted pipe. Still no sign of Todd. I made soup that day; someone else made dinner. Todd came and ate dinner at the house that night, but he didn't want a bed.

In the morning, we found Todd at work in the kitchen as usual, but his speech was slurred, and he was weaving a little. He looked sad and he talked to no one. We all pretended not to notice that he was drunk, everyone knowing that anyone who broke the silence would have to ask Todd to leave. Finally, someone mentioned that Todd was drunk. It was one of the guests; I can't remember which one, but I remember feeling like kicking the guy out for thirty days—punishment for putting into words what everyone knew already. Instead I agreed to talk to Todd.

Before I could begin the standard rap ("Todd, if you're loaded, and all the other guys know that we know you're loaded . . ."), Todd stopped me. "I know. I ain't no different from these other guys." There were all sorts of things I wanted to say. That he was a *lot* different from these other guys. That we didn't love him in that terrible, cold way we "love"—which means "tolerate"—our "guests"—which means "the bums we tolerate." I wanted to tell him that he reminded all of us of our fathers and grandfathers, that he was special to all of us, that we needed him and loved him and cared that he was screwing himself up hopelessly. I wanted to beg him not to drink, since to ask him to leave would crush us all.

What I did say was: "Okay, Todd. As long as you understand. You'll have to take off, now."

A few days later, one of the guys saw Todd, drunk and quiet, waiting near a viaduct. He was going to hop a freight bound for Denver. None of us has seen him since.

The things laypeople have to go through to become saints!

When it was discovered that Cecilia, a Roman girl of the patrician class, had not only converted to Christianity, but had consecrated her virginity to God, in the process converting her fiance, Valerian, to the new sect, the prefect ordered that she be stifled to death in the bathroom of her own house. Three days of steam and heat failed to kill her, and the soldiers assigned to execute her grew impatient. After three clumsy blows, they despaired of beheading her and left her to die. She lingered for three days more.

Probably around the same time, a Gallic officer of the Imperial Guard became a Christian. Sebastian was sentenced to be used as a target for archers he had formerly commanded. He apparently was a poor archery teacher, since they finally had to beat him to death.

But it could be that the story of Zaccheus, chief among Jericho's publicans, speaks more to our age than all the dramatic violence of martyrology. By climbing a sycamore tree to get a glimpse of Christ, the little man allowed himself to appear ridiculous. That took guts—the laughter of the crowd was for him the cross.

Facile cynicism, the stuff you see written in the *National Lampoon,* the smug implication that wisdom is the realization that there is no wisdom . . .

these are probably the deadliest powers of the Flesh these days.

To be murdered for the Faith, to die for a cause, any cause at all, at least promises a sort of remunerative historical glow. Maybe terrorists embrace violence to be assured that no one will laugh at their cause. If I hijack a plane, threatening to murder old men, women and children unless the Beatles agree to regroup for a concert in Fargo, North Dakota, people's attention won't be focused on the absurdity of my demands but on the horrible thing I might do.

But if I started a public fast on the steps of Capitol Records' offices, refusing to eat until the Beatles had regrouped and promised to play in Fargo, I wouldn't be dangerous. I'd be nuts, and treated accordingly.

The problem is that this age has taught us to believe that nothing matters. (Or that, if anything matters, it has something to do with the most bewildering statement Vince Lombardi ever made: "Winning isn't everything; it's the only thing." If that nonsensical statement means what I think Vince meant it to mean, he could have erased the first part of it, in which case the Packers and the Black Septembrists would have a common creed.) Anything which you embrace with your whole life, whether it be Amway or the Gospel, appears silly and unless you're willing to kill people for it, you appear as silly as your cause.

So when a friend of mine was recently arrested on the steps of the Pentagon for pouring blood on its pillars and defacing government property, I reacted with the wisdom of our age. I said he was nuts. True, he was acting courageously, prayerfully, and non-violently. The spilling of blood was a liturgical act, a confrontation of the Beast in its own lair, armed only with the imperative of the Gospel. But the act didn't break the spell the times have woven around me, and I still find myself thinking that his protest was melodramatic and foolish. But what else could he do? The same spell couldn't be broken by Pope Paul, when he spoke to the United Nations on nuclear weaponry:

> Let these shameful weapons be banned. Let this terrible art, which consists in manufacturing, multiplying and storing bombs to terrorize the people . . . be outlawed. The obvious contradiction between the waste involved in the overproduction of military devices and the extent of unsatisfied vital needs is in itself an act of aggression which amounts to a crime, for even when they are not used, by their costs alone, armaments kill the poor by causing them to starve.

Everyone must have been sleeping. He was applauded wildly, said Mass at Yankee stadium, and flew away. Nobody but Catholic Worker-types, lunatics who throw blood at the Pentagon, seemed very impressed.

We don't scourge, crucify, or exile our prophets anymore. We ignore them, or give them our attention, and then laugh.

Ignatius of Antioch begged his followers in Rome not to appeal for his reprieve. He was anxious to be torn apart by the beasts in the arena. My friend spent thirty days in jail, and people laughed at him. One of the mysteries of the Faith is that both Ignatius and my friend suffered the same lunacy, and that lunacy is redemptive.